Digital Blood on Their Hands

Cyberattacks are nothing particularly new to the world and Ukraine had suffered many such attacks by Russia over recent years. Russia had knowingly been exploiting Ukraine's digital vulnerabilities as a proving ground for nearly a decade. Malware such as Sandworm and BlackEnergy had caused untold damage to the Ukrainian population and government previously and allowed Russia to perfect cyberattacks for further, more global events. Russia had been planting cyber sleeper digital cells for years, especially in the US and the UK.

Then, coincidently, the week after the Chinese Winter Olympic games had finished, Russia launched an all-out cyber offensive against 70 Ukrainian government websites. Owing to these being poorly—and insecurely—maintained, they toppled one by one, causing havoc and disruption to the Ukrainian government and to Ukraine's critical infrastructure. As Q said in James Bond: 'I can do more damage by breakfast sipping my Earl Grey tea with my keyboard than you ever can in the field.' Sadly, Q was right, as we witness daily. The keyboard and mouse have indeed become mightier than the sword.

The barrage of cyberattacks against Ukraine constitutes the first cyberwar by one nation against another. This attack crossed a very thin red line. That line had the hallmarks of a nation state, but had until now been confined to cyber criminal activities, immaterial of whom the perpetrators were. This, however, was now *war*. The cyberwar was simply a precursor, the softening of a country that would precede a kinetic war in which tens of thousands of people would lose their lives. This war was the first war for nearly 80 years that rang out deathly klaxons across Europe and the world.

Digital Blood on Their Hands addresses the issues that the digital world has created, covering the culpability, causal links and even liabilities that go towards these war crime atrocities, often too frightening to believe and also too compelling to dismiss. It tells a side to the world's first ever cyberwar that you would never otherwise see, or possibly hear about.

Digital Blood on Their Hands
The Ukraine Cyberwar Attacks

A. J. Jenkinson

CRC Press
Taylor & Francis Group
Boca Raton London New York

CRC Press is an imprint of the
Taylor & Francis Group, an **informa** business

Cover Image Credit: Shutterstock.com

First edition published 2023
by CRC Press
6000 Broken Sound Parkway NW, Suite 300, Boca Raton, FL 33487-2742

and by CRC Press
4 Park Square, Milton Park, Abingdon, Oxon, OX14 4RN

CRC Press is an imprint of Taylor & Francis Group, LLC

ISBN: 978-1-032-34668-7 (hbk)
ISBN: 978-1-032-34669-4 (pbk)
ISBN: 978-1-003-32327-3 (ebk)

DOI: 10.1201/9781003323273

Typeset in Minion
by KnowledgeWorks Global Ltd.

Disclaimer

The views and opinions expressed in this book are the author's own and do not necessarily reflect the views of CRC Press, Taylor & Francis Group, or Informa, or any employees of these companies. The author, A. J. Jenkinson has made all reasonable efforts to ensure that the information presented in this book is fair, accurate and comprehensive.

Contents

Preface

March 2022

On Thursday 24 February 2022, coincidently, the same day as my sister's birthday, Russia launched a comprehensive invasion of Ukraine. This attack followed weeks of Russian forces building on the Russian–Ukrainian border, amidst dismissive rhetoric by Vladimir Vladimirovich Putin, Russia's President of a 'special operations exercise' and weeks of cyberwar attacks on critical digital infrastructure.

What made this war markedly different from any other war in history was its use of cyberwar as a precursor to the kinetic war that followed some five weeks later.

Russia launched a cyberwar offensive against Ukraine and, although the methods and attacks were nothing particularly new in their use and deployment, it was the sheer scale and debilitating nature of over 70 Ukraine government websites and infrastructure that caused chaos across many normal Ukraine government channels.

Attacks such as Man-in-The-Middle (MiTM) and no doubt code injections to enable domain admin access and domain hijacking and takeover were witnessed. Although such attacks are nothing particularly new, as these followed closely in the fashion seen in 2020 when SolarWinds suffered similar digital intrusions, using near identical methods with the same outcomes, it was the scale and audacity that was shocking and crippling.

What is more, it also heralded a major milestone that other governments' own basic security negligence also left them highly exposed. That thin red line had undoubtedly been crossed and would threaten every government and country globally as, unlike a warhead with a limited range, cyberattacks have no boundaries or limits and due to security negligence, even gross negligence, every critical infrastructure globally could be targeted and infiltrated.

The modus operandi had been set over the last two decades or more. However, although growing in frequency and scale, the attacks had, until now, been confined to cybercriminals looking to sell data to anyone willing to pay. This had created an entire black market cyber ecosystem all the way up to and including zero days, where no 'fix' is yet known or developed.

Just as in the Cold War, Russia had been taught well by its 'opponents', namely the United States of America. The US invested billions of taxpayers' money in a quest to ensure digital supremacy, knowing full well that whoever could control the digital world would indeed have a major advantage over the rest of the world, not only from a commercial but also from a military perspective. Warfare had now moved on from land, air and sea to include cyberwar.

On mid-January 2022, Russia launched a bombardment of cyberattacks upon insecure Ukraine government websites and infiltrated at least 70 of them. This included the Ukraine's military and even Ukraine's cyber command centre. But how and what was Russia's desired outcome? Clearly, it was to cause havoc, chaos and destabilise the entire country.

We had already commenced threat intelligence gathering on numerous Ukraine government websites and had tried to inform the various people there, eventually getting to communicate directly with one of their third-party US partners and alerting them to just some of the oversights and errors. On 18 January 2022, we exchanged genuinely concerning information on numerous Ukraine government websites. One example was www.mfa.gov.ua, which is the Ministry of Foreign Affairs for Ukraine and connected, as you would expect, to numerous other government websites.

The MFA (Ministry of Foreign Affairs) government website was displaying a 'not secure' text in the uniform resource locator (URL) address bar due to a public key infrastructure (PKI) error and issue. This meant it was not only easily identified as being 'not secure', but it also confirmed basic security was lacking and therefore not only could it be easily abused, but it also confirmed data was being sent to and from the server in plain text (unencrypted). I will explain more on this later, save to say, the data was not encrypted due to the PKI issue, an expired and invalid digital certificate. We identified dozens of other Ukraine government websites with the same errors, rendering them also 'not secure' and exploitable.

When we started peeling back the layers, you will hear the term 'defence in depth', which means exactly that. You cannot—or certainly should not—rely on a single secure position, but multiple ones. In terms of defence, the Ukraine government and its technical partners failed the basic security, that of perimeter defence, by making errors that would nullify all other levels of security, no matter how complex, how many millions or even billions was spent and, when these errors are made, wasted.

Such basic security errors, as happened to SolarWinds in 2020, mean that, once infiltrated, nobody can see or notice them as metaphorically the enemy is now masquerading as one of the internal team by wearing the same uniform. These basic security errors are not only confined to the visual errors of PKI, invalid digital certificates by displaying the 'not secure' text on the website, but also the domain name system (DNS), which is where the content is handed to a content delivery network (CDN) to distribute that data, globally if required. It is imperative that this is also *secure*.

In the case of Ukraine government websites that were successfully attacked as part of the Russian cyberwar offensive and a precursor to the kinetic war, they were not only 'not secure' for the world to see, but also their *side* and *backdoors* were wide open to enable and even facilitate infiltration, unbeknown to everyone until the attack became known sometime later. That is, of course, unless it was planned.

It is not beyond the realms of possibility that this cyberwar was months, even years in the planning as part of the Russian overall reconnaissance to identify insecure digital targets. We have identified insecure positions that dated from at least August 2019 that would enable 'sleeper digital plants and cells' to have been implanted ready for activity. It is also not beyond the realms of possibility that data was being captured, controlled and amended for several years due to these basic security errors.

As I write this preface on 23 March 2022, the basic security errors are *still* in place and the US tech third-party insists on going via attorneys instead of directly engaging to address their security oversights and gross negligence. Do they have something to hide? Quite possibly. Are they complicit by being complacent? We cannot speculate at this point. All we can confirm is that the Ukrainian government and thousands of other organisations are highly exposed due to their basic security errors.

I can confirm that finally, on 16 March 2022, Ukraine's website www.mfa.gov.ua had a valid digital certificate placed upon it at 00:00 UTC. This is some eight weeks after we first informed them of the basic security error. However, the DNS is still completely exposed. This situation, as mentioned, nullifies all other security measures, including this digital certificate.

On Wednesday 26 January 2022, the White House released a paper titled: 'Moving the US Government to a Zero Trust Model'. It is an extremely useful and insightful document and was published only nine days after the Russian cyberwar attacks commenced upon Ukraine and cites DNS no fewer than 47 times. Is this perhaps a coincidence? With years of experience, we have become somewhat battle hardened and we rarely subscribe to coincidences in the cybersecurity world.

The ongoing Ukraine cyberwar and war are both currently raging. The invasion has seen the exodus of millions of Ukraine's citizens, predominantly women and children as men under 60 are forced to stay and fight. The war has so far claimed the needless loss of lives on both the Russian and Ukraine sides in their tens of thousands and with predicted losses of as many of 1 million people due to the war and lack of food and water. In this war, no matter how it started or who is culpable, time will show basic security measures aided and even facilitated the war, which marked the beginning of what we all hope does not escalate to become a chemical or even a nuclear war.

I would personally like to applaud the citizens of Ukraine for their courage and determination. The fact that far too many leaders of the world have allowed such a situation to manifest itself is an utter disgrace and, eventually, those responsible *must* be held to account.

Digital Blood on Their Hands fills in the blanks. It will inform and enlighten everyone of how we got here, and where we will hopefully go and what we need to do to alter the destructive course we are currently on. You will no doubt have heard the term, 'I hope it was not all in vain', this I truly hope by my addressing and bringing the real world of clandestine cyberwar and cyberattacks to be openly discussed and addressed, not just by ignorant politicians looking to achieve their next vote so they manipulate their view of the world and vastly increase their personal bank balances, but to serve the citizens of the world congruently and as a collective. Less of me, and more of us.

Governments, the Intelligence Community—including the alphabet agencies—are at a major crossroads. Do they continue manipulating the cyber realm without any defence by focusing on purely offence, the same offensive capabilities as we are witnessing against Ukraine and now Russia, or do we start taking security, basic security, seriously?

We have frequently been marginalised because of our views, beliefs and knowledge. It is often considered 'dirty little secrets' that are best left unsaid due to fear of reprisals to politicians or tech giants signing the next multi-billion dollar deal, which provides no more security, and instead of mitigating, adds to the already woefully exposed positions. Smoke, mirrors and sleight of hand is being used by Wall Street building security unicorns, not to better protect the citizens of the world, but to line their bulging, dirty pockets further.

Personally, I am sick to my stomach of the tech giant forcing our hand to use attorneys as literally thousands upon thousands of people are dying either directly or indirectly, quite possibly due to their errors. The title of this book, *Digital Blood on Their Hands*, could not be more apt.

Author

A. J. Jenkinson is CEO of Cybersec Innovation Partners. He has eight years' risk, compliance, and cybersecurity experience. Before taking on that role, for 20 years he was CEO of Charterhouse Risk and Compliance. There, he led a team starting with zero to more than 500 technical experts, including leading a program for Sun Microsystems as a client for nearly 10 years, as well as other government contracts. After publishing his first books, *Stuxnet to Sunburst* and then *Ransomware and Cybercrime*, Andrew was subsequently made a Fellow of the Cyber Theory Institute and acknowledged as a thought leader in the field of public key infrastructure and domain name systems, the fundamental basics of all security. He has also been named as one of the world's 30 leading cyber security experts by the European Institute of Risk.

Other books by this author:

Stuxnet to Sunburst: 20 Years of Digital Exploitation and Cyber Warfare https://www.routledge.com/Stuxnet-to-Sunburst-20-Years-of-Digital-Exploitation-and-Cyber-Warfare/Jenkinson/p/book/9781032068503

Ransomware and Cybercrime https://www.routledge.com/Ransomware-and-Cybercrime/Jenkinson/p/book/9781032235509

I

History

CHAPTER 1

The History of War and Cyber Warfare

O N 17 JANUARY 2022, modern warfare changed, and it will never change back again. Russia's cyberwar on Ukraine is an unprecedented event in the history of warfare. The war launched by Russia follows a long history of war. Let us briefly explore the history of war and cyber warfare to give some context to the history of these events and this technology.

Throughout recent decades, governments have supported what has become known as the intelligence community (IC). These groups covered various areas and included the FBI, the CIA, MI5, MI6 and the like. This has expanded to include groups like the National Security Agency (NSA), created on 4 November 1952 and Government Communications Headquarters (GCHQ), created some time earlier on 1 November 1919. Both have tried to adjust their expertise, and both are shrouded in a degree of secrecy. Both agencies played their digital intelligence hands decades ago, often without the full knowledge or sanction of their respective governments, let alone considering what might occur should their digital manipulation and abuse were copied by cyber criminals.

The history of war can be described as an intense armed conflict between states, governments, societies or paramilitary groups. The forces can include mercenaries, insurgents and militias.

Warfare is literally as old as civilisation itself. It is often believed that the first conflicts date back 10,000 years in Syria, Jordan and Iraq. Wars over

DOI: 10.1201/9781003323273-2

land, resources and goods were the rationale for these conflicts, which some 10,000 years later seem very similar and little different.

There have been many civil wars, also known as intrastate wars. Civil wars are conflicts between groups within the same state or country. These can be categorised as:

- Ancient and early medieval, prior to 1000

- Medieval, from 1000 to 1600

- Early modern, from 1600 to 1800

- Modern, from 1800 to 1945

- All wars from 1945 onwards

Throughout history, there have been hundreds of wars, possibly thousands. Wars, for some, are good business. If you are a munitions manufacturer or supplier, it is often very lucrative and of course fuels the entire war machine. Politics always plays a critical part in war and, as a race, human beings have typically been all too willing to join in confrontation. Add beliefs, religion, resources and even treasure, and it does little to stem the aggression and cease hostilities.

Typically, all wars have included extreme violence, aggression, destruction and loss of life. An example of this that is still fresh and well-known is the Second World War. The Second World War cost, in today's terms, US$4 trillion and over 70 million people perished as a direct result. Let me repeat that: 70 million people perished. That is the same as every man, woman and child that lives in the UK killed in what can be considered as one man's quest and obsession. At the time, the total population of the world was 2.3 billion people, so the total killed from 1939 to 1945 represented around 3 per cent of this number.

During the Second World War, GCHQ played a critical role within the top-secret area, which also included the most famous decryption of the encryption machines, namely the Enigma and Lorenz cipher machines. Both Alan Turing and William Tutte worked directly for the agency at Bletchley Park to 'crack the code' that each machine created. Encryption and decryption will constantly come into play and nowhere more so than in cybersecurity.

Often overlooked and often ignored was the fact that one line in every coded message the Nazi's sent was the single line, 'Heil Hitler'. This egotistic line was the same in every message, no matter what code or syntax was used, so finally that line gave the encryption code away on each message.

Encryption dates back to Egyptian times as one of the earliest forms using symbols which were found in the tomb of Khnumhotep, who lived in 1900 BC. Without the 'key' to decryption, it was virtually impossible to decode the message.

Encryption, decryption and cyberwar are now part of the world landscape. Encrypted WhatsApp messages, signal messages and even emails are supposed to be encrypted using public key infrastructure (digital certificates and encrypted keys) to identify the devices and users. It is here at the 'hand-off' that things break down and why many specialists in the sector term the monster being turned against its creator. This area of hand-off is often abused and termed as a 'Man-in-The-Middle' (MiTM) attack.

Let me explain further and share a little of the history of what has become modern cyber warfare.

On 29 October 1969, when the Internet was new and emails only a pipe dream, the very first message was emailed. The message was sent LO. Connection was lost before the entire message was sent, LOGIN. LO become affectionally known as 'Lo and behold'. This message marked the beginning of modern communications and, although initially designed for universities and academics so they could share findings and research for the betterment of humanity, the commerciality could not be—and was not—ignored.

Coincidently (although, as mentioned, we do not subscribe to them) exactly 50 years later, on 29 October 2019, Cybersec Innovation Partners was recognised as one of the top 10 cybersecurity firms in the UK by the government organisation Tech UK.

Fast forward from 1969 to 2001 when lots of things had happened, and the US IC groups were transitioning, with many struggling from the days of the Cold War, to move into the digital age. The 9/11 terrorist attacks on the New York Twin Towers called for a massive focus, as well as funds, to take control of the digital realm.

Only several months before the Twin Tower atrocity, in May 2001 Jim Gosler, director of Clandestine Information Technology, and who became known as the godfather of digital offensive capability, said upon his retirement from the CIA: 'Either the Intelligence Community would learn to adapt, or the Internet would eat them alive'. Profound words most certainly.

President Bush called numerous, urgent meetings with the IC and demanded digital supremacy. Billions and billions of dollars were signed off for programmes with weird and wonderful names, often without any known deliverables or explanations to Congress. Funds were simply signed off and that continued under President Obama.

My first book, *Stuxnet to Sunburst, 20 years of Digital Infiltration* covers this period in more depth. However, back in 2008, Stuxnet was the name given to the digital attack that used and manipulated digital certificates to plant malicious code to cause collateral damage at Natanz, the Iranian Nuclear facility. This was *not* termed an act of war, surprisingly; however, it did cost many lives, and certainly could be considered as such from any other viewpoint, causing huge collateral damage. Attribution in cyberattacks still remains a very grey area.

The first known cyberattack is often attributed to Robert Morris, a 20-something Cornell graduate student when he inadvertently released a 'worm' that quickly clogged up large sections of the Internet. However, it would be some time later that cyberattacks and ransomware would become daily events.

Around 2010, cyberattacks were becoming more commonplace and the revelations by Edward Snowden shortly thereafter confirmed just how invasive and comprehensive the NSA, CIA and GCHQ, among others, had been to ensure that *all* digital traffic was visible and able to be captured, and then harvested by the IC teams. Remember, this started out with what is believed to be the best intentions to identify terrorist cells and to eavesdrop upon them digitally in order to prevent terrorist plots and to thwart such attacks. However, it quickly became too intoxicating for the agencies to discriminate, and they simply took all available data to harvest. Originally, this had been only the case if the call had originated from or was going externally to the US. Now it included every device and every person. If it had an Internet protocol (IP) address and was connected, it was good enough to capture the data.

Remember too that Facebook started on 4 February 2004. One of the original investors was the CIA, in confirmation of George Orwell's *1984* predictions about Big Brother, which simply became a reality. More recently, the Swiss global government encryption machine providing company, Crypto AG, who supplied 120 governments with encryption machines and capability, was found to have been complete with extras. Those extras were backdoors—built-in methods of bypassing the security of a system—designed and built-in by Crypto AG's owners, the CIA. It is easy to see to what lengths the IC—including the CIA—would go to ensure they captured all the data and would process it accordingly as they saw fit. Think having a backdoor in the original Enigma machine or typing your password in whilst someone is making a copy.

You may be asking what all this has to do with the cyberwar in Ukraine. Well, before 2001 Jim Gosler's team that he headed up at the CIA were developing offensive capabilities. These included capabilities that enabled them to gain what would be, to any other mortal, illegal access to personal computers (PCs), phones and devices via Internet connections.

You will be familiar with the term remote access. Well, it is not just for an engineer to reboot a system. It can, and does, enable remote access and potentially command and control (C2) of that device, the servers that device might be connected to, and the network thereafter. That little plug in to a laptop, PC, even TV and now IOT device enables digital eavesdropping and offensive capabilities.

Remote desktop access (RDA) or remote desktop protocol (RDP) is often responsible and used to gain control over a computer or even a network. The Oldsmar water treatment cyberattack was a classic example when an unpatched computer enabled RDA and the attacker attempted to alter the water chemicals (Sodium Hydroxide) parts per million to a dangerously high, potential life-threatening level. The attacker's actions were thwarted only by good fortune by a fellow engineer who noticed that the cursor on the adjacent screen was moving, whilst nobody was sitting at the machine.

Access via a computer, website, email, server, DNS or CDN are the areas to monitor and control. Lacking governance in any of these areas undoubtedly causes the vast majority of digital infiltration.

CHAPTER 2

The History of Cybersecurity

THE TRUE BIRTH OF cybersecurity occurred in the 1970s. This began with a project called the Advanced Research Projects Agency Network (ARPANET). This was the connectivity network developed and the precursor to the Internet itself.

A chap named Bob Thomas discovered and determined it was possible for a computer program to move over a network. As it did so, the program would leave a trail as it moved. He developed the program so that it could move between the Tenex terminals on ARPANET.

Mr Thomas called his program Creeper. Thomas created the program to carry and then to print a simple message. *'I'm the creeper: catch me if you can.'*

This sparked much interest and some concern. It was this message that also spurred a man named Ray Tomlinson to develop a new program. He called this program Reaper. Tomlinson, who gained fame for his development of email, developed Reaper to chase, and then delete, Creeper.

Reaper was the first example of an antivirus software program. It was also called a self-replicating program. That made Reaper the world's first computer worm. At this time, computer technology continued to grow and expand. Most networks relied on telephone systems for connectivity: you will remember those wonderful bleeps, bangs and noises. This would place ever-increasing, new and a higher level of demand on ways to secure the networks. Every piece of hardware connected to the network created a

DOI: 10.1201/9781003323273-3

new type of entry point. These were vulnerabilities in the network. Access to any cybercriminal is key: no access equals no crime.

The development of security solutions was even more important at this point. Governments began discussing ways to address and reduce these vulnerabilities. Governments also learned that unauthorised access across their ever-increasing networks and systems could create numerous problems. A range of scientific papers was written in the second half of the decade examining ways to provide this security. These papers also detailed the risks that were prevalent and expected to occur.

The Electronic Systems Division (ESD) of the US Air Force Command began working on projects. The Advanced Research Projects Agency (ARPA) was also involved. It was a division of the US Defence Department. Their task was to develop security for the Honeywell Multics (HIS level 68) computer system. Other organisations began working on network security as well. That included the Stanford Research Institution and UCLA.

The Protection Analysis Project from ARPA was a key component of development. It looked at a wide range of topics including identifying vulnerabilities. It also worked on various aspects of operating system security. It also aimed to develop automated methods for spotting vulnerabilities in software programs. All of these were new topics and insights in the industry and chartered new territory.

By the mid-1970s, a true development of cybersecurity was growing. It was now necessary for computer developers, for the first time in history, to focus on creating safe and secure systems. Security would always play second fiddle to functionality.

In 1979, just as the decade was drawing to a close, the first cybercriminal was arrested. His name was Kevin Mitnick. Kevin was just 16 years old, something of a coincidence in light of the recent arrest in the UK of the 16-year-old teenager found to be behind a ransomware gang near Oxford. Kevin had managed to hack into the Ark. The Ark was a massive system that was used for developing operating systems (OS). The Ark was located at the Digital Equipment Corporation. Mr Mitnick managed to make copies of the software after gaining access to it (nothing much has changed about gaining access). He was captured for his actions, arrested and jailed for the illegal access and crime. This event marked the start of literally thousands upon thousands of cyberattacks in the coming decades.

With the advent of cyberattacks, the 1980s brought numerous and increasing challenges for computer networks. A number of high-profile attacks would take place throughout the decade. These would include attacks on AT&T, the Los Alamos National Laboratory and National CSS. It was in 1983 that new terms were developed to describe these attacks. Among them were 'computer virus' and 'Trojan Horse', or Remote Access Trojan or RAT, as it would later become known.

In 1983, the domain name system (DNS) was created by Dr Paul Mockapetris and became one of the original Internet standards a few years later in 1986 once the Internet Engineering Task Force (IETF) was created. Two documents marked the start of DNS, namely RFC 1034 and RFC 1035. They described the entire protocol functionality and included the data types that they could carry. I consider myself to be very blessed to have spoken and swapped notes with Paul recently.

DNS is still as critical as ever, if not even more so today due to the sheer scale of the Internet and domains, as well as the 'fashion' to outsource and use content delivery networks (CDNs) such as Akamai, AWS (Amazon Web Services), Cloudflare and so on.

Dr Paul Mockapetris and his team were tasked with the challenge and mission to make the Internet user friendly. That entailed making text into binary numbers and vice versa for people and computers not to be forced to remember a sequence of numbers which computers happily work with but people do not. Over time, this became a decentralised model and worked perfectly well until a number of people realised that they could gain access via the DNS and especially when the DNS was assumed to be secure. Remember public key infrastructure (PKI) at this point may have been known and even used by certain agencies; however, it would be another decade before digital certificates and encrypted keys would be used in the mid-1990s to identify and authenticate users and devices. The Wild West has been around in the technology world for decades, as everyone, or the vast majority of people, learnt on the job.

A big fear at the time was the threat from other governments. It was still the middle of the Cold War. The move from analogue espionage to cyber espionage was very real, although digital espionage offered ease of access and the ability to eavesdrop digitally from literally thousands of miles away. It forced the US government to create new guidelines and resources for managing such events and threats. The Trusted Computer System Evaluation Criteria was developed in 1985 by the US Department of Defence. It was later called the Orange Book.

This guide was invaluable as it was one of the first guides for the security of computers. It aimed to assess how much trust could be placed on software that used different types of sensitive information. It also established basic security measures that software manufacturers needed to consider. This would create a foundation from which commercial computer programs were developed in terms of cybersecurity and truly spawned an industry. It also was too attractive for the agencies and governments not to capitalise upon and build backdoors into. The definition of a digital backdoor is typically a covert method of by-passing normal authentication and encryption of a computer without the owner's or user's explicit knowledge or permission.

The threat was real. A man named Marcus Hess, a hacker from Germany, managed to infiltrate the government's systems in 1986. He used an Internet gateway located in California. As I have already said, nothing much has changed and access back in 1986 used an Internet gateway exactly as the Russians used to gain access to Ukraine government websites in 2022. To do this, he managed to piggyback onto ARPANET. The result was astounding. In what seemed to be a matter of minutes, he was able to access some 400 military computers. Among those were the mainframes being used by the Pentagon itself. He planned to sell all of the information he gathered to the KGB. Digital infiltration and data exfiltration are the same: identical models are used now, decades later, for cybercriminals attacking organisations with ransomware attacks.

This was a time of new (digital) toys to play with, a playground for adolescents and young adults exploring new worlds.

The attack left many companies wondering what to do. It seems many still have the same dilemma. At some point, security became a bigger focus. Information and strategies for mitigating such risks were being developed. For example, one big trend was the need to monitor the size of the command.com files being sent. The larger the file, the more likely it was of catching a virus or other risk. Of course, that did not remain the case.

Think of digital data in terms of sending mail. If you send a postcard, anyone can read it. If it is in an envelope, there is a degree of obfuscation. Equally, as you send your physical packet via a Post Office, DHL or FedEx, you expect the packet to be delivered from A to B in an identical manner as to when it was sent. Digital data is identical to ensure security. If the packet is altered in anyway on its journey in the digital world, it is a sure sign that the connection between A and B is *not* secure. The repercussions of such alteration can mean the difference between life and death.

Another sign was a drop in accessible memory. If that occurred, it could signal an infection on the computer system. Today, a slowdown in a computer is still a sign that malicious activity is likely to be occurring. The latter part of the 1980s saw the real development of the cybersecurity industry. Commercial antivirus products were first developed and released in 1987, just a year after the Pentagon attack.

What is confusing is knowing who developed the first product. Many claims exist. Some of the most notable to consider include the development of VirusScan, a product developed by John McAfee, who went on to found his own company with the same name. An antivirus product was released for the Atari ST by Kai Figge and Andreas Luning. Around the same time a no drive antivirus solution was released in Czechoslovakia as well.

Bernd Fix—who is just a month younger than me—took on the challenge of the Vienna virus. This virus was one of the first forms of malware to be created. It spread through systems and corrupted files as it went. Mr Fix was able to address and remove the virus successfully.

This was also the year of the Cascade virus. Cascade was one of the first encrypted viruses. It moved through and infected. com files. While the virus itself was considered harsh, it is also important to mention that it also spurred the development of new antivirus solutions. Cascade successfully managed to infect the computer systems at IBM.

The development of the computer worm also flourished in the 1980s. Many believe Robert T. Morris developed it. He was a student studying at Cornell University and wanted to determine the size of the Internet as a whole. To do it, he built a worm in 1988. The worm's goal was to move through and infect UNIX systems. When infected, it would count the connections present on the web. The Morris Worm was a self-replicating virus.

Mr Morris' plan did not work well. An error in the design of the program caused it to infect each machine, one after the other. This led to networks that were clogged with information, leading to massive crashes. The program was aggressive and eventually left the Internet slowed down. What makes this particular event important is that it was one of the first widely publicised events in cybersecurity. It would certainly not be the last.

This worm was unique in the way it was written, too. It was the first to exploit system vulnerabilities. Mr Morris was also the first person to be charged under the Computer Fraud and Abuse Act. The worm he developed led to the development of the Computer Emergency Response Team (CERT). The event also sparked a change in cybersecurity itself. More people were investigating and researching how to create deadlier and more effective worms and viruses. The more people developed these problems, the more they evolved and became more invasive. To counteract this, there was an increasing need to develop new antivirus solutions that could respond rapidly to these problems.

By the end of the decade, there were numerous antivirus solutions on the market. These included Norman Virus Control, ThunderBYTE and F-Prot. IBM also released its previously internally used product to the public. It was one of the first IBM VirusScan and MS-DOS solutions.

The 1990s witnessed the incredible growth and development of the Internet. The cybersecurity industry tried and failed dramatically to grow with it. The cybersecurity industry is always many steps behind and often playing Whack-a-Mole as it tries to keep pace.

Polymorphic virus risks developed. In 1990, the first code that mutates as it infects PCs that also keep the original algorithm in place was developed. The polymorphic virus was designed to avoid detection. That made it harder for computer users to know it was even there.

The DiskKiller virus was released by *PC Today*, a magazine aimed at computer users. It infected thousands of computers. The magazine edition offered the disc to subscribers. The magazine's owners stated that it was an accident, and they did not know the risk was present. The first anti-virus program was developed.

In the mid-1990s, PKI was rolled out globally. PKI is a set of rules, hardware, software and procedures needed to create, manage, distribute, use, store and revoke digital certificates and mange public-key encryption. The purpose of PKI is to facilitate the secure electronic transfer of information for a range of network activities such as ecommerce, Internet banking and emails. PKI was originally developed by the Intelligence Community and agencies for their own information sharing and was deemed useful for the entire digital communications of the world. At what point it was misused and abused is unclear; however, misused and abused it was, no doubt with the aid of the certificate authorities, who were subsequently awarded lucrative government contracts.

In 1996, stealth capability was further developed. This was also the same year that macro viruses were released. Both created more challenges and required new developments of antivirus software. From the first antivirus onwards, the goal was to increase ways to protect against risks. As one hacker group developed after another, companies faced huge challenges to improve security in order to minimise data breaches.

More types of malicious programs were on the way. The ILOVEYOU virus and Melissa infected millions of computers in the 1990s, targeting Microsoft Outlook in particular. These viruses caused significant slowdowns and failures of email systems. The I LOVE YOU outbreak was estimated to have cost US$10–15 billion globally to remove the worm, which is virtually no longer seen. The Pentagon, CIA and the British government closed their entire email systems to address the cyberattack. Around this time, many of the existing viruses circulating were seeking financial gains. Some were aimed directly at strategic organisations. There were ever-increasing instances in which individuals suffered data loss, financial loss or other risks due to these viruses. Major news reports picked up on such attacks at a rapid pace. That rightly led to more pressure to create cyber security solutions. Computer security was growing and becoming big business as a result.

Over the following years, new strategies were developed to help with ever-increasing problems. One of these was secure socket layer (SSL), first introduced by Netscape in 1994. As the Internet continued growing at a rapid pace, there was an urgent need for transport security for web browsers and for various transmission control protocols (TCPs). It was developed as a way of protecting users who were moving across the Internet. SSL was put in place in 1995. It helped to protect activities like online purchases. It would later be the foundation for the development of hypertext transfer protocol (HTTP), which was superseded by hypertext transfer protocol secure (HTTPS) in 2018 and was, to all intents and purposes, upgraded due to Google taking the lead and campaigning from 2013/14 for its global adoption in 2018. At that point, any website not using HTTPS and the latest protocols would display the now infamous 'not secure' text in the address bar.

This move also saw any website relegated in the search engine optimisation (SEO) league. When a website displays the 'not secure' text typically followed by http://example.com instead of https://example.com, it is a sure sign and giveaway that the website is insecure and potentially exploitable. I had shared several Ukraine government websites displaying the 'not secure' text with Microsoft's Head of Ukraine and Ukraine government, many of which were attacked as part of Russia's cyberwar offensive programme prior to the kinetic war on 24 February 2022, some five weeks later. We discuss this in more detail elsewhere in this book.

No matter what the changes have been over recent decades, one thing is constant, and that is that cybercriminals and even cyberwar attacks require access. Perversely, 2018 will not only go down in history as the year HTTP was upgraded to HTTPS (Secure), but also the year that notified cyber criminals of who, and who had adopted the new secure protocol, and who, by default had not. Those that did not made for easy targets to exploit. Google wanted to embarrass organisations to do the right thing, although it would seem that many organisations did not receive the memo and are still 'not secure' some four years later. This includes many that have already been hacked.

By displaying a 'not secure' text, the website confirms that not only was the latest version of HTTPS not being used but it also confirmed that certain ports might be open. This questions the integrity of the website, the integrity of the data, both at rest and in flight, and it also confirms that the data in flight could be captured and read in plain text—that is to say, the data are unencrypted—which is exactly why HTTP was upgraded to HTTPS in order to enforce encryption.

It has become all too apparent that cybercriminals love plain text data. They can infiltrate, exfiltrate and encrypt the data and hold the company to ransom to release the company encryption key to enable the data to be used often in a matter of minutes. Reactive security is all but worthless.

Again, perversely, companies, now in panic mode, will do more, often much more, to regain control of the data that their oversight and negligence resulted in and that they were charged with securing and protecting once taken, rather than actually doing the job properly in the first place. The simple truth is we did *not* write the rules; however, those that choose to overlook, ignore them—and, by rules, we are referring to the basics of security: DNS, and PKI—do so at enormous risk. We have researched over 1,000 cyberattacked companies and organisations, and every one of them had PKI or DNS issues, often blatantly so. This was not a percentage or a high number, but all of them—every single one.

It has been said by many people that it is more a case of when rather than if a company will suffer a cyberattack, and one cannot easily argue that fact. I would go even further and say that any company overlooking or ignoring its DNS and PKI areas is certainly at the very top of a hacking list. Similarly, any company that displays a 'not secure' text on its website makes itself a prime target and is displaying to the world that it lacks all security controls and capability and will know little or nothing about being attacked in the first place.

The analogy I often use as a former international sportsman is that you do not go to a training session or gym in the hope of achieving anything. It is something you must work on and become disciplined at. The more you put in, hopefully the more you will get out. Cybersecurity is the same; it requires discipline and consistent effort. The areas in which we witness most errors being made are DNS and PKI. In the last year or so, more and more agencies are focusing on releasing videos and papers, and that includes the White House and the European Commission on DNS abuse and attacks.

One final word on this. It does not matter how many millions of dollars are spent or how big the security team is. If DNS and PKI are ignored, every dollar spent on security is wasted and negated due to ignoring the foundational basics of all security and facilitating very backdoors that are supposed to be there to ensure correct security. Often, that is the DNS and CDN's error as much as the parent company. Vigilance and discipline are unequivocally required.

II

Technology

II

Technology

CHAPTER 3

Domain Name System (DNS) Attacks

DOMAIN NAME SYSTEMS (DNSs) are often considered the phone book of the Internet. The full explanation of DNS is as follows: the DNS is a hierarchal and decentralised naming system used to identify computers, services and other resources reachable through the Internet or other Internet protocol (IP) networks. The resource records contained in the DNS associate domain names with other forms of information. In simple terms, people can use and recall the alphabet more easily than a string of numbers. Computers only use numbers. As such, when computers 'speak' to each other and share data, they do so by sharing numbers. People can remember www.google.com better and more easily than 142.250.189.238, for example.

DNS came into being as far back as 1983 and became one of the original Internet standards in 1986 after the creation of the Internet Engineering Task Force (IETF).

A content delivery network (CDN) or content distribution network is a geographically distributed network of proxy servers and their data centres. Remember, there is no Cloud; it is simply someone else's computer. The ability of a CDN is to provide high-quality availability and performance by distributing the service spatially relative to end users. CDNs have been around since the late 1990s and their demand grew digitally as the world was seemingly shrinking.

DOI: 10.1201/9781003323273-5

If we think of both DNS and CDN as having collection and distribution capability, we can think of DNS as being the digital equivalent to millions of letters, parcels and so on, and a CDN as being the digital distribution channels like DHL, FedEx, UPS and so on.

A major difference, however, is that the Internet, knowingly weaponised for decades, has cyber criminals constantly looking for easy access; that is, where the 'hand-off' of content by a parent company to its DNS and CDN providers is. If insecurely managed, that data is at heightened risk of being captured and used for nefarious purposes, even exploited as part of an overall cyberwar offensive.

Worse still, if the CDN provider such as Akamai, Amazon Web Services (AWS), Cloudflare, Fastly, or one of many others, lacks basic security itself, this can provide simple backdoor access and, sadly, frequently does so whilst going completely unnoticed. We call this 'Living off the Land'. The 'sophisticated' card is typically played, and everyone looks to blame the Chinese, Iranian, Korean or Russian cyber groups for the audacious intrusion. It is always easier to blame others rather than hold one's hand up by confessing to basic security oversight and negligence that is really culpable.

In most cases, the CDN manages—and is supposed to control—the DNS. One CDN provider suggests that a parent company—its client, lest we forget—should check its Internet facing security, which includes its DNS and CDN positions, every 12 hours. We certainly subscribe to this thought process, unlike the highly questionable security professional who suggested web checks should be taken as part of an annual pen test. What happens during the remaining 364 days each year does not seemingly matter then.

We categorise access via websites as being predominantly via PKI or DNS misconfigurations, oversights or errors, invalid or mismatched digital certificates, or insecure DNS positions. In such cases, a savvy cybercriminal—or even a 16-year-old teenager, for that matter—can easily identify and just as easily infiltrate. Cries of Computer Misuse Act (CMA) mean truly little as we are talking criminals here. Any website displaying 'not secure' identifies the organisation as being complacent when it comes to basic security and lacking basic security. It typically follows that internal security is also lax and that access can be easily and simply gained. Unfettered access to the network, data and much more is an easy task and can be all the way up to command and control.

Ever since its creation in 1983–1986, DNS was acknowledged as one of the most critical Internet protocols, period. It is the key component that allows a computer to show content, right before your eyes, including email services and chat services. Even social networks rely on DNS to work 24 hours a day, seven days a week resolving IP addresses into hostnames.

Yes, DNS really is that important, and that critical. It is therefore rather disappointing, even shocking that it is one of the most overlooked elements and protocols when any organisation performs a security hardening of its infrastructure. This is when DNS-based attacks happen and because many organisations do not realise DNS is a critical attack vector. It is often found without proper protection, outdated or completely vulnerable. Those in any doubt, or are unsure, please read this paragraph again.

There are many types of DNS attacks. All have the same outcome, and that is to achieve access and to cause disruption and chaos. The different types of attack include the following:

- Domain hijacking (SolarWinds as an example)

- Domain flood attacks

- Distributed reflection denial of services

- Cache poisoning

- DNS tunnelling

- DNS hijack attack

- Random SUBDOMAIN ATTACK

- NXDOMAIN attack

- Phantom domain attack

Let us look further at the different types of attacks and how they can affect online presence.

DOMAIN HIJACKING

This type of attack can involve changes in DNS servers and domain registrar that can direct traffic away from the original servers to new destinations.

Domain hijacking is often caused by many factors related to exploiting a vulnerability in the domain name registrar's system and can also be achieved at the DNS level when attackers take control of your DNS records.

Once the domain name is hijacked, it will probably be used to launch malicious activities such as setting up a fake page of payment systems like PayPal, Visa or bank institutions. Attackers will create an identical copy of the real website (Evil Twin) that records critical personal information such as email addresses, usernames and passwords. We have previously identified Spoof PayPal pages and notified PayPal of these.

DNS FLOOD ATTACK

This is one of the most basic types of DNS attack. In this distributed denial of service (DDoS), the attacker will hit DNS servers. The main goal of this kind of DNS flood is simply to overload servers so they cannot continue serving DNS requests, because the resolution of resource records is affected by all the hosted DNS zones.

This kind of attack often comes from one single IP. However, it can get difficult when it becomes a DDoS, where hundreds or thousands of hosts are involved.

While many requests will be instantly detected as malicious, many legal requests will be made in order to confuse defence mechanisms. This makes the mitigation system job a little bit harder sometimes.

DISTRIBUTED REFLECTION DENIAL OF SERVICE

When it comes to DDoS, the rules change in order to diffuse the source of the attack and enable it to be distributed across a large number of hosts. The ultimate goal of any DDoS is to overload a network with a large number of packets or a large number of bandwidth-consuming requests, either to overload a network capacity or to exhaust hardware resources.

The difference between DDoS and distributed reflection denial of service (DRDoS) is the act of making any target unavailable by denying its online services with flood requests. The DRDoS is a little bit different, and often more effective.

A DRDoS attack will try to send requests from its own servers, and the trick lies in spoofing the source address that will be set to that of the targeted victim, which will cause all machines to reply back and flood the target.

This kind of attack often involves and is generated by botnets that run compromised systems or services, which will ultimately be used to create the amplification effect and attack the target.

CACHE POISONING

DNS cache poisoning, also known as DNS spoofing, is one of the most common DNS attacks that happens daily. The trick in this kind of attack is very easy to understand. By exploiting system vulnerabilities, attackers will try to inject malicious data into DNS resolvers' cache. This is an attack technique often used to redirect victims to another remote server.

Once the cache poisoning attack is live, attackers will receive all the legitimate traffic in their own servers, which are often used to show phishing-based pages to steal personal information from visitors. This is a very common attack that has seen the likes of British Airways and the German Government lose hundreds of millions in costs and losses.

DNS attacks work because most of the time they are caused, and enabled by, exposed and vulnerable DNS records. Opening spam emails containing malicious links can expose you to a system compromise, and ultimately get your DNS resolver cache modified to lead you finally to malicious websites in order to steal your personal information or infect you with spyware, adware, viruses, etc.

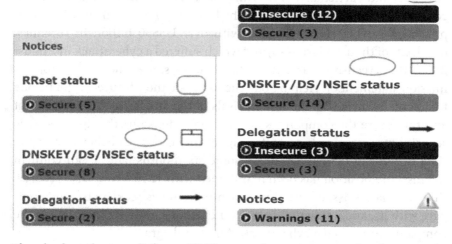

If we look at the two different DNS scans above, we see a tale of two vastly different results. The DNS record scan on the left shows a solid set of secure results with five secure DNS records, eight secure DNSKEY and two secure delegation. The DNS record scan on the right shows a vastly different story: one of total insecurity. We can see 12 insecure DNS records. These include web facing (A), mail exchange (MX), named servers (NS), start of authority (SOA) and text (TXT). The latter is used to verify domain names and detecting forged domain names that are used for spam or phishing emails.

There are three insecure delegation issues and 11 warnings. The two DNS record scans above could not be any different and they confirm several things. The first is the company on the left clearly take its security seriously; equally, that reflects well on its overall security, both external and internally. It also confirms that, in order to hack this company, it will take much more than a casual oversight or 'drive by' with easy access.

The second company on the right shows that basic security control and overall security is totally lacking and that can be expected to be part of their overall security posture. It also confirms that, should a cyberattack be launched, after accessing the organisation, the chances are that nobody will notice, as nobody is looking or checking. Such security oversight, negligence and incompetence also flag the organisation up to any would-be cybercriminal as an easy target and as easily exploited using any one of a plethora of available attack methods.

I have trimmed the DNS record scan results above so they are anonymous; however, I can confirm they are both from 2021. The screenshot on the left is an exception; the screenshot on the right, although particularly bad, and particularly concerning, is sadly not uncommon. I can also confirm the screenshot on the right belongs to a global, leading, self-proclaimed cyber security leader with over US$50 billion in revenues, hundreds of thousands of staff, and which suffered a cyberattack in August 2021—the screenshot was actually taken at the same time. The company's mission statement of 'Helping our clients create their future' might be one that actually bites it as the full reprisals of the attack are still playing out and the future the company is helping to create is one that ignores basic security measures, only to suffer digital intrusions. Unbelievably, at the time of writing (28 March 2022), some six months later, I can confirm the insecure position has been maintained with 12 insecure DNS records, three delegation issues and three warnings. This is reckless beyond compare with its, and its clients', security. Remember, only six months ago the company announced a cyberattack. An utter disgrace.

Domain Name System Security Extensions (DNSSEC) are a suite of extensions that add security to the DNS protocol by enabling DNS response to be validated. Specifically, DNSSEC provides origin authority, data integrity and authenticated denial of existence. DNSSEC has been around for under a decade; however, it addresses many of the basic issues that are often overlooked or ignored.

We always suggest that companies that make themselves targets by displaying 'not secure' websites are committing the cardinal sin of security.

Equally, when global Chief Information Security Officers (CISOs) do *not* know that their secure socket layer (SSL) digital certificate is worthless when their DNS is compromised or the incorrect digital certificate is being used, or even when hypertext transfer protocol (HTTP) is not correctly redirecting to hypertext transfer protocol secure (HTTPS) is nothing short of reckless, even scandalous. Such a false sense of security is rife across many industries and egos abound, leaving thousands of companies and governments totally exposed.

We appreciate the task in hand takes discipline, knowledge and continuous action. It *must* become a habitual habit if an organisation is ever to fend off cyberattacks and digital intrusions. Sure, it is tough, but wait until the sickening feeling of having all your personal data stolen and used, causing massive challenges to your personal life, then let me know how that feels.

I leave the reader with this thought. DNS, like PKI and CDNs thereafter, were used, and exploited in the very early days by government agencies for favours and government contracts and the like. There is obviously a reluctance to declare this as fact; however, it is one of the worst kept secrets globally in the security industry. The rationale was security and protection against wrongdoing and in governments' attempts to identify terrorists. It rapidly grew into full-scale population monitoring and data harvesting for many areas, indeed, virtually every area. It is hard to identify exactly when cybercriminal activities utilised the same methods; however, PKI and DNS are two massive areas that are being continually exploited today.

The focus by government agencies over the last five decades or so, especially the last three, has seen a total focus on offensive capabilities. As mentioned above, DNS first appeared in 1983, nearly 40 years ago. On 26 January 2022, the White House released its paper on moving the US government to a zero trust model and cited DNS 47 times. In the last few years, the Cybersecurity and Infrastructure Security Agency (CISA) has made videos and written papers on the subject of DNS. The sceptics amongst us might easily believe that the agencies are trying to warn the digital world some 30 years too late, after much damage and devastation has been done.

Whichever way it is looked at, these basic, fundamental security errors are costing the global economy trillions of dollars annually and destabilising our way of life as rarely witnessed before. The ongoing cyberwar and kinetic war are continually exploiting these security errors at government level and will continue to do so until these areas are addressed and remediated.

For the want of a digital certificate. . .

CHAPTER 4

Content Delivery Networks (CDNs)

ONTENT DELIVERY NETWORKS (CDNs) HAVE really started to reveal their true power recently and usefulness, even though they have been around for decades. An insight into how CDNs came to be is quite useful. CDNs can be considered surrogate web servers distributed across different data centres around the globe and in different geographical regions to deliver content to end-users, based upon the proximity of the user. Using a CDN hosting provider enables reach, removal of latency issues, and typically offers a cost-effective solution for web content distribution for online vendors and e-commerce owners and to enable a global presence as many organisations require $24 \times 7 \times 365$ uptime. This, of course, has numerous challenges, some of which will be addressed shortly.

Using a CDN prevents latency issues, meaning faster performance of a hosted website and (hopefully) better security from cyberattacks. This is because CDNs maintain multiple points of presence, i.e., servers store copies of identical content (domain name system (DNS) records) and apply a mechanism that provides logs and information to the origin servers. Instead of a standard client–server communication, two communication flows are used, first between the client and the surrogate server, and then between the surrogate server and the origin server.

As I have written throughout this book as a firm belief of mine, where you can find joints you can find weaknesses. We tend to bundle up DNS and CDN provision as the same and it is not unusual for a CDN to control

DOI: 10.1201/9781003323273-6

and manage all DNS records. This is a major area of responsibility, and one that is *not* always managed well.

The development of CDNs sought to deal with the increase in Internet usage and the explosion of websites, along with the extreme bandwidth pressures. The first video stream was growing the demand as well as the number of content providers. That was in the past. Now, CDNs are a continual trend, and with the emergence of cloud computing, involving all the layers of cloud computing, including the following:

- SaaS (Software as a Service), e.g., Google Docs

- IaaS (Infrastructure as a Service), e.g., Amazon

- PaaS (Platform as a Service) e.g., Google App Engine

- BPaaS (Business Process as a Service) e.g., advertising, payments, etc.

An early diagram of CDN can be seen below:

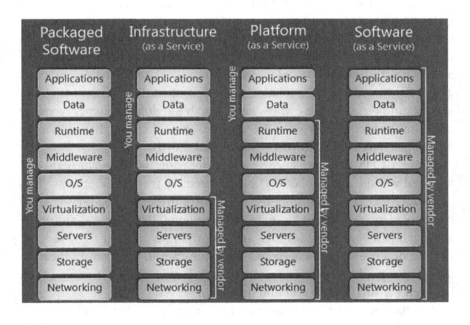

The first generations of CDNs were seen in the late 1990s. However, there were some technological innovations that preceded this generation of CDNs, such as server farms, hierarchical caching, caching proxy deployment and so on. These developments were crucial for paving the ground of the designed and desired infrastructure of such Internet to speed up and unclog technology. Bandwidth was always a major consideration.

Early CDNs were designed initially to address the increased demand for audio and the new video streaming, to reduce latency of websites' content loading, and to support growing volumes of content. Finally, the CDNs were to enable the companies' providing products or services to handle the ever-growing requests from the Internet, digital users, and to provide a major benefit by removing the need for in-house capability and geographical spread of servers. Remember, the Big Sale was not only global reach, but perceived cost reduction due to moving costs onto operating costs away from capital expenditure, which afforded better profits to be shown and enjoyed in all its forms. There were significant savings for IT teams and budgets, reducing overall costs for IT infrastructure.

The main focus of the second generation of CDNs, however, was a peer-to-peer production, cloud computing and energy awareness. Green views have sold well for the last few decades, of course. CDNs were also serving the demand of the Internet crowd for more interactivity, not only from their desktop browser, but also from mobile devices. Many Internet service providers (ISPs), telcos, IT companies and traditional broadcasters spread across the globe. Some moved into the CDN industries themselves (Amazon, AT&T and many more).

The third generation of CDNs is expected to be completely community driven, autonomous, and self-manageable. Its main focus is on the quality of experience for the end-user. Throughout the 1990s, the adoption of cloud computing and CDNs usage grew rapidly; however, none more so than in the last decade. There were significant historical events that drove the market, few more so than the desire by government agencies to pool data in a centralised manner. Other noteworthy events that sped up the adoption of cloud and CDN were the 9/11 terrorist attack: a sudden, unanticipated mass of Internet users tried to access the particular news site simultaneously. This caused severe caching problems, and finally more money invested in developing CDN hosting to provide protection from the flash crowds for the websites.

Akamai Technologies evolved out of a Massachusetts Institute of Technology (MIT) research effort aimed at solving the flash crowd problem. Broadband Services Forum (BSF), ICAP forum, Internet Streaming Media Alliance organisations all led initiatives to develop standards for delivering broadband content, streaming rich media content—video, audio and associated data—over the Internet.

By 2002, large-scale ISPs started building their own CDN functionality, to provide customised services. In 2004, more than 3,000 companies were found to use CDNs, spending more than US$20 million monthly. In 2005, CDN revenue for both streaming video and Internet radio was estimated to be growing at 40 per cent. The combined commercial market value for streaming audio, video, streaming audio and video advertising, download media and entertainment was estimated at between US$385 million and US$452 million in 2005. In 2008, Amazon launched its own CDN. In 2011, AT&T announced its new cloud-based CDN that enabled content to flow from its 38 data centres around the world to reduce transit and latency times.

In May 2011, Google said it had 200,000 active applications and 100,000 active developers. The stocks of leading CDN market players (Akamai, Limelight, EdgeCast) slumped; Akamai's total revenue for 2011 was US$1,159 million, a 13 per cent increase over 2010 revenue of US$1,024 million. Akamai's stock revenue for 2012 is reported to be US$345.32 million. Cisco projected 2012 Video CDN revenues at around US$1 billion, with growth for 2013 between 40 per cent and 45 per cent, and the complete market to grow from US$6 billion to US$12 billion by 2015.

According to Markets and Markets, the CDN market by Component (Solutions, Web Performance Optimisation, Media Delivery, Cloud Security and Services) will grow from today's US$19.2 billion to US$34 billion by 2027 at an annual compound growth rate of over 12.5 per cent. The presence of key players in the ecosystem has led to a competitive and diverse market. CDNs are an interconnected system of computers on the Internet that provide web content rapidly to numerous users by duplicating or caching the content on multiple servers and directing the content to users.

CDNs are used by an exceptionally significant percentage of Internet users today, including web objects, text, graphics and scripts, downloadable objects, media, files, software, documents, applications, eCommerce, portals, real-time streaming, data, on-demand streaming media and so on. When an Internet user requests a specific web page, video or file, the server nearest to that user is determined and is subsequently used to deliver that content. Content may be replicated on hundreds or even thousands of servers to provide identical content to as many users as possible.

It goes without saying, then, that just as content can be distributed concurrently and to potentially thousands of computers, the same can be said when security is compromised and that any insecure position could affect not just a single computer or server, but hundreds, thousands, even millions.

When we started researching the cyberwar attacks on Ukraine government websites on the 17/18 January 2022, we discovered some genuinely concerning issues. These issues highlighted public key infrastructure (PKI) issues, DNS issues and CDN issues.

We immediately reached out to the Ukraine government and its third-party suppliers who were also insecure and, although we did exchange several emails, nothing was actually addressed or remediated apart from finally, on 16 March 2022, a replacement digital certificate was placed on www.mfa.gov.ua for a year. Prior to that, it had languished as one of dozens of Ukraine government websites that were 'not secure'. I can confirm that, as of 31 March 2022, the major security errors are still being ignored and maintained.

We continued our research and trying to reach out to Ukraine government entities, including its cyber command, which also was managing an insecure website, but to no avail. These also remain insecure due to third-party PKI errors.

What our extensive research clearly evidences is that not only are Ukraine government websites insecure, but so are many more; in fact, millions more organisations have insecure websites due to fundamental, basic PKI security errors that impact every one of the millions of clients that use the third-party services.

Our research looked at numerous other CDN providers and what we discovered was systemic, planet-scale errors in PKI and DNS that unknowingly, or knowingly, remain open to interpretation. However, it is a well-known industry fact that government agencies initially manipulated PKI and DNS in order to eavesdrop digitally. Another less well-known fact is that cybercriminals have, over the last several years and decades, replicated the exact same methods used and perfected by the agencies. The motives may be vastly different; however, the outcome of digital intrusion is remarkably similar. The end game is also radically different.

There is also much confusion, even amongst security professionals. They may well be more generation Y than generation X and, as such, grew up with less exposure to DNS and PKI, which may have been considered yesterday's security fashion and news and only understandable and used by data scientists and cryptographers. Human nature typically pushes back when there is a lack of knowledge and, in a later chapter, I will demonstrate this when the Chief Information Security Officer (CISO) of

Lloyd's of London denied the relevance or importance of DNS and PKI issues to the overall security as he waived a secure socket layer (SSL) security test, declaring Lloyd's was secure. As Winston Churchill said: 'I love learning, but I hate being taught'. Never a truer word was spoken.

I read recently that the Australian government has declared an A$9.9 billion budget for Australia's Signals Directorate (ASD), which, on the face of it, is excellent. However, to put things into perspective, that figure is lost to cybercrime daily, and even more across the world. In addition, Australia, even though it is one of the Five Eyes, has nothing short of pathetic basic and fundamental security. We have tried to help at Australian government level, its Department of Defence, and even its critical infrastructure and all have done little but to bury their heads in Manly Beach. Australia remains a melting pot of easy, exploitable targets, as is true of many governments, organisations and countries that continue to overlook and ignore DNS and PKI.

Let me ask this. Do we think this A$9.9 billion will directly prevent cyberattacks in Australia? The answer is no, absolutely not, as the very fabric of security is flawed, fundamentally vulnerable and exploitable due to eyes being shut, ears being covered and mouths tight-lipped. In a conversation three years ago with the head of the Department of Defence (DOD) in Australia, Karl Hanmore, he said: 'Andy, you are perfectly correct. Australian companies, including government, are totally missing basic security, unfortunately, we can only advise, not enforce.' I shared a 'not secure' Australian DOD homepage with Karl, as well as many others, including the Reserve Bank of Australia. No further action was taken save for the extrapolation of taxpayers' dollars for more *false* security and rhetoric, which continues to this day, as this sheer waste of A$9.9 billion testifies to.

By ignoring and not addressing these issues people are complicit with cyberattacks due to being complacent. When evidence is shared and still ignored, we are not simply talking negligence, but gross negligence which carries not only damages, but punitive damages. It is an incredibly sad indictment that we have tried tirelessly for years to help educate and provide DNS and PKI knowledge, only to witness ignorance and complacency across many sectors, industries, and even governments.

As Mark Twain said: 'It's easier to fool people than to convince them they have been fooled.'

CHAPTER 5

Cloud Computing

A Gamble?

CLOUD COMPUTING IS THE on-demand availability of computer system resources, especially data storage and computing power, without direct active management by the user. Large clouds often have functions distributed over multiple locations, each location being a data centre.

In 1963, the Defence Advanced Research Projects Agency (DARPA) presented Massachusetts Institute of Technology (MIT) with US$2 million for Project MAC. The funding included a requirement for MIT to develop technology allowing for a 'computer to be used by two or more people, simultaneously'. These were the days of those gigantic, archaic computers using reels of magnetic tape for memory that became the precursor to what would go on to become what we collectively know as cloud computing. It acted as a primitive cloud with two or three people accessing it. The word virtualisation was used to describe this situation, although the meaning of virtualisation would later be expanded.

In 1969, JCR Licklider helped to develop the Advanced Research Projects Agency Network (ARPANET), the forerunner of the Internet. JCR, or Lick, was both a psychologist and a computer scientist, and he promoted a vision called the 'Intergalactic Computer Network', in which everyone on the planet would be interconnected by way of computers and be able to access information from anywhere. (What could such an unrealistic, impossible-to-pay-for, fantasy of the future look like?) The Intergalactic Computer Network, otherwise known as the Internet, is necessary for access to the cloud.

DOI: 10.1201/9781003323273-7

The meaning of virtualisation began altering in the 1970s. It now describes the creation of a virtual machine, that acts like a real computer, with a fully functional operating system. The concept of virtualisation has evolved with the Internet, as organisations and large technology giant businesses began offering 'virtual' private networks as a rentable service. The use of virtual computers became popular in the 1990s, leading to the development of the modern cloud computing infrastructure. The timing of the domain name system (DNS) and private key infrastructure (PKI) is not coincidental as, although the entire drive of moving to virtual machines was seen to be by commercially savvy entrepreneurs, it was very much driven by the governments and their agencies to capture data and collate in fewer locations to harvest and trawl through.

In 1997, Professor Ramnath Chellapa of Emory University stated that cloud computing was the new 'computing paradigm, where the boundaries of computing would be determined by economic rationale, rather than technical limits alone'. This description describes the cloud's evolution suitably.

Throughout the 1990s, cloud computing gained popularity as companies started to better understand its services and usefulness. In 1999, Salesforce became a popular example of using cloud computing successfully. It was used to pioneer the idea of using the Internet to deliver software programs to the end users. The program (or application) could be accessed and downloaded by anyone with Internet access. Businesses could purchase the software in an on-demand, cost-effective manner, without leaving the office.

Cloud computing also had the massive benefit of taking capex (capital expenditure), moving it off balance sheets, to opex (operational expenditure), which afforded lower 'fixed costs' and enabled better profitability to be shown, which in turn enabled greater profits, at least on paper. This in turn enabled higher bonuses. Cloud computing was only going one way and that would lead to further challenges and major security issues.

Remote access to computers had been in existence since the 1980s and was called carbon copy. The software was originally developed and produced by Meridian Technologies, which used a trick to stay resident in the memory of disk operating systems (DOS). This allowed remote users to call in and manage a computer via a phone line. Remote access became a firm favourite, initially with the government agencies, but more latterly with cyber criminals. One of the more recent, genuinely concerning events and display of remote access was the Oldsmar Water Treatment takeover, when remote access enabled a nefarious actor to change the Sodium hydroxide from 100 parts per million to 11,100. If it had not been for an engineer noticing the cursor of the neighbouring personal computer (PC) screen moving, who knows what could have happened.

There is a significant risk faced by organisations' cloud infrastructure and that is unauthorised access to data and data breaches. According to cloud security spotlight report, unauthorised access via incorrect access controls and misuse of employee credentials, via social engineering, or similar, is the single largest threat.

Although there are several approaches that are behind cloud security breaches, immaterial of the root or access, the outcomes are the same. The cloud provider and company's reputation is damaged, and customers may leave in droves. It does, of course, depend upon the 'sophistication' of the attack (forgive my attempt at humour). Cloud breaches have far surpassed what is known as on prem (on premises).

According to several publications, the seven largest and most destructive cloud cyberattacks are as follows:

1. *Yahoo.* In 2013, Yahoo suffered a massive cyberattack that went unnoticed until 2016. It still ranks as one of the most devastating breaches due to the sheer scale and numbers. The company initially announced that 1 billion customers were affected, that number swelled to over 3 billion accounts. The attack commenced with a spear-phishing email campaign. One click and boom. In 2017, four people were indicted by the FBI, two of whom were Russian spies.

2. *Alibaba.* In 2019, Alibaba (the Chinese shopping goliath)'s website Taobao suffered a cyberattack that lasted eight months. Some 1.1 billion pieces of data were impacted and due to the fact this attack was in China, the full details were suppressed and will most probably never be made public.

3. *LinkedIn.* In 2021, over 700 million LinkedIn profiles fell victim to a data scraping breach. Much of the information that was scraped was public. However, the data was posted on the Dark Web and exposed. Although LinkedIn denied and debated responsibility it was not the first, nor will it be the last for a social media site, professional or otherwise, to fall victim to basic security oversights and errors.

4. *Sina Webo*. One of China's largest social media platforms with 600 million users was hacked in June 2020. The company announced that the personally identifiable information (PII) data of some 172 million users had been stolen. It is unclear how the original attack occurred; the data was put on the Dark Web for sale.

5. *Facebook*. In August 2019, and only announced some time later in April 2021. Whilst Facebook stated that it had fixed the problem; Mark Zuckerberg was called before the Federal Trade Commission to face fines up to US$5 billion.

6. *Marriott International*. In September 2018, an attack that had lasted for four years following the acquisition of Starwood's by the hotel group saw Marriott retain the booking system, not knowing the booking system had already been hacked and continued to be so for four years. The number of people affected totalled hundreds of millions, including all their PII data. This was particularly sensitive as government agencies all used Marriott as they had a country-wide agreement. As such, much of the Intelligence Community had their PII data compromised which, along with the Office of Personnel Management (OPM) in 2013/2014 was something of a double blow.

7. *Adult Friend Finder*. In October 2016, more than 412 million user accounts from multiple sites were exposed. In 2016, it had the dubious claim to be the year's largest hack. The data included all PII data, with far-reaching consequences for those affected. The hack is believed to have used a local file exclusion exploit enabling hackers access to all network sites.

Cloud computing is attractive to cybercriminals due to the consolidated data accessible in one fell swoop. It is also attractive to government agencies due to the data capturing and harvesting of that data to enable social understanding and management.

Amazon introduced its web-based services in 2002. It was a first for a major business to think of using its capacity as a problem to be solved. This went on to become known as the cloud computing infrastructure model and gave Amazon the flexibility to use its own computers' capacity more efficiently. This started something of a revolution in cloud computing and Amazon's competitors and peers were quick to follow suit.

By 2006, Amazon had launched Amazon Web Services (AWS), which offered online services to other websites and clients. AWS provided a variety of cloud-based services, including storage, computation and intelligence. One of AWS's sites was the Elastic Compute Cloud (EC2). EC2 allowed organisations and individuals to rent virtual computers and use their own programs and applications.

In the same year, Google launched the Google Docs services. Google Docs was originally based on two separate products Google: Spreadsheets and Writely. Google had purchased Writely, which offered individuals the ability to save documents, edit and transfer them into blogging systems and—an Internet-based program that allowed users to develop, update and edit spreadsheets, and then to share the data online. An Ajax-based program is used, which was compatible with Microsoft Excel. The spreadsheets could be saved in an HTML format.

In 2007, IBM, Google and several universities joined forces to develop a server farm for research projects needing both fast processors and huge data sets. Remember that academia had been instrumental in the early days of ARPANET, which would become the Internet. The University of Washington was the first to use the resources provided by IBM and Google. Carnegie Mellon University, MIT, Stanford University, the University of Maryland and the University of California at Berkeley quickly followed. These universities soon realised computer experiments could be done much faster and at reduced costs. IBM and Google supported their research. Much of the research was directly addressing problems IBM and Google had interests in and, as such, they benefited enormously from the collaboration. 2007 also saw the launch of Netflix's streaming video service. Netflix used cloud and supported its customers with the practice of binge-watching.

Eucalyptus, which had started out in academics, had a solid business plan for making its 'infrastructure as a service' open-source platform the centre of the cloud-computing universe. Eucalyptus started to offer the first AWS API compatible platform, which was used for distributing private clouds, in 2008. In the same year, NASA's Open Nebula provided the first open-source software for deploying private and hybrid clouds. Many of its most innovative features focused on the needs of major businesses. Eucalyptus stated in 2009: 'It is reasonably clear that open source is the heart of cloud computing, with open-source components adding up to equal cloud services like Amazon Web Services. What is not yet clear is how much the cloud will wear that open source on its sleeve, as it were.'

Private clouds were initiated as far back as 2008. However, they were still undeveloped, and adoption was mixed. Remember that computing in essence was simply being outsourced to someone else's computer and not with much control, and frequently questionable security. Concerns with poor security in public clouds was a strong driving force promoting the use of private clouds. We will come back to this. In 2010, companies like AWS, Microsoft and OpenStack had developed private clouds that were certainly functional; after all, these were simply their data centres that required connectivity. OpenStack in 2010 also offered its open-sourced, free, do-it-yourself cloud, which became very popular, and available to the general public.

The concept of hybrid clouds was introduced in 2011. We use hybrid as a word frequently today for vehicles of course in a similar way. A fair amount of interoperability was required between private and public clouds, along with the ability to shift workloads back and forth between the two. Very few businesses had systems capable of doing this at the time, although many wanted to, because of the tools and storage public clouds could offer, along with the early mentioned perceived economies of scale, the capex/opex benefits and, besides, these companies were *not* seen as computer organisations, although they all heavily relied upon and were indeed dependent upon computing capability. Finally, it also perversely removed some of their security responsibility, or so the common thought process and belief would have executives believe.

In 2011, IBM introduced the Smart Cloud framework, in support of Smarter Planet, which was a cultural thinking project. Then, Apple launched the iCloud, which focused on storing more personal information (PII data) as well as music, pictures and so on. Microsoft began using the cloud on television for advertising, ramping up the general public's awareness of its ability to store photos or videos with easy access to migrate and store to its cloud service.

Oracle introduced its cloud service in 2012 and offered three basics for business: IaaS (Infrastructure-as-a-Service), PaaS (Platform-as-a-Service) and SAAS (Software-as-a-Service). These services and offerings quickly became the new norm, with some public clouds offering all of these services, while others focused on offering only one. Software-as-a-service, which was widely adopted, becoming very popular.

CloudBolt was founded in 2012. This company gets credit for developing its hybrid cloud management platform, which helped organisations build, deploy and manage both private and public clouds. CloudBolt resolved many of the interoperability challenges between public and private clouds. CloudBolt is still pushing hard within the cloud space today.

Multi-clouds began when organisations started using SaaS (Software-as-a-Service) providers for certain services, such as human resources, customer relations management and supply chain management. This started becoming popular from 2013 into 2014. The use of SaaS providers is very popular, a model of using multiple clouds for their specific services and advantages has developed. This philosophy enables flexibility and avoids becoming trapped using a specific cloud because of interoperability problems.

By 2014, cloud computing had developed its basic features, and security had become a major concern, as the list of cloud providers suffering cyberattacks was concerningly increasing. Cloud security had become a fast-growing service, because of its importance to customers. Cloud security advanced significantly over the last few years, or so Cloud providers would have you believe. If you believe the hype and blurb, the Cloud was providing protection comparable to traditional IT security systems. This included the protection of critical information from accidental deletion, theft and data leakage. Security should always be the primary concern of most Cloud users. Sadly, as the evidence below shows, it rarely does and quarterly targets, commission, bonuses and shareholder dividends take centre stage long before REAL security does.

Currently, one of the primary users of cloud services are application developers. In 2016, the cloud began to shift from developer-friendly to developer-driven. Application developers began taking full advantage of the cloud for the tools it offered. A large number of services strive to be developer-friendly to draw more customers. Realising the need, and the potential for profit, cloud vendors developed (and continue to develop) the tools app developers wanted and needed.

The above is a snapshot of the history of cloud computing and an overview of how it came into being. Never forget that government agencies, let alone cloud providers themselves were more than happy to charge for their services and to capture data in one place. This afforded them much more control and capability to use the data from a single captured source.

We have quoted several companies, and major ones at that, who provide cloud services globally. We have confirmed that much of cloud computing was formed and relied upon open-source capabilities and indeed used open-source to its benefit.

In 2019, the global cloud computing market was valued at US$266 billion and was predicted to expand at a compound annual growth rate (CAGR) of 14.9 per cent from 2020 to 2027. Conservatively, then, that puts the cloud market at well over US$300 billion per annum, or around US$25 billion per month, making it just shy of US$1 billion per day. It is fair to say that cloud computing for the vast majority of providers is a fantastic and lucrative business.

The question we pose, and that every user and every citizen should pose is, apart from declaring security is important, why is that statement hollow and without substance?

The three screenshots of Amazon, Cloudbolt and IBM, all major cloud providers evidences that, on Wednesday 30 March 2022, all three had *insecure* zones.

To confirm, if the DNS record shows numerous insecure positions, which can include web facing (A), canonical name (CNAME), mail exchange (MX), named server (NS), start of authority (SOA) or text (TXT) record, these are all exploitable and enable Man-in-The-Middle (MiTM) attacks, amongst many others. When the DNS record zone shows as *insecure*, it means everything that sits or is connected to the top domain is *insecure*. This not only should sound alarms, but klaxons. It certainly undermines and compounds all other security measures and, without reading the small print within specific contracts, we would suggest that service level agreements (SLAs) along with moral and legal responsibilities may lie with each cloud provider.

As Dr Paul Vixie, a DNS leading authority says: 'A DNS Zone that is Unsecure is Bad, really bad.' I can confirm that, as of 25 July 2022, all three of the above DNS zones are identical and have *insecure* DNS zones.

It is apparent—and quite possible—that cloud providers' security teams fall more into Generation Y than Generation X and simply skipped the whole PKI and DNS waves in the 1980s and 1990s. However, as the basis of all security relies upon both, it might be a really useful idea to get someone who does actually know both, as it is clearly evident that these three cloud providers, and many others, have PKI and DNS issues rendering them, and critically importantly, their millions upon millions of clients exposed, vulnerable and exploitable. It is also clear from our research that these cloud providers have maintained their *insecure* positions for many months, some for many years.

For brevity, we have not included cloud and content delivery network (CDN) providers such as Akamai, Cloudflare, Fastly and dozen of others. It is safe to say that our research showed that none—not one—of these providers has strong basic PKI and DNS security. This basically confirms (well, certainly to us, at any rate) that decisions made upon selecting a cloud provider rely *100 per cent* upon zero checks of any security provided or adopted as part of any due diligence. It also confirms that if you put rubbish and insecure data in, add more rubbish and insecure data, the output is more rubbish and more insecure data and output. Just as you cannot go onto a 'not secure' website and then become secure after going to different pages, no amount of security features will override the *insecure* zone. Nothing.

Cyberattacks and cyberwars will continue to rage not because cyber criminals have become more intelligent, or more sophisticated; they have simply learnt how to better identify and exploit the security errors and negligence that is exposed by organisations, including DNS, CDN and cloud providers.

CHAPTER 6

OSINT

Open-Source Intelligence

M ODERN DAY OPEN-SOURCE INTELLIGENCE surprisingly owes much of its resurgence to Iran. Iran has more online users than Bahrain, the United Arab Emirates (UAE), Israel, Saudi Arabia, Syria, Yemen and Jordan combined. During the last Revolution, Matthew Weaver at *The Guardian* expressed surprise at the realities of this new world: 'What people are saying at one point in the day is then confirmed by more conventional sources four or five hours later.' This was in 2016.

Open-source intelligence (OSINT) has its roots sometime earlier, however. It was in upstate New York, 1883 where open-source intelligence really commenced. It was there that one of the US intelligence's most influential figures was born. William Donovan was the son of devout Irish immigrants and grew up in a working-class family. William excelled himself at school and academia.

Donovan had an ambition and that was to become the first Roman Catholic President of the United States—nothing too lofty then. He did sometime later come close to the Presidency as in 1905, Donovan went to Columbia Law School, where one of his classmates was none other than a young Franklin D. Roosevelt.

After fighting in the first World War, Donovan became a lawyer and enjoyed a very successful career. Donovan narrowly missed becoming the Attorney General in 1925. Throughout the interwar period, Donovan

DOI: 10.1201/9781003323273-8

travelled the world as a lawyer, meeting influential foreign figures and authored reports for the US government, in a semi-official capacity.

Donovan's connection to FDR led to the creation of the first intelligence agency in the United States. Until that time, the world of intelligence and spying was seen as highly questionable, even ungentlemanly. Donovan lobbied his former school colleague FDR to formalise his 'unofficial' work for the US government and, on 11 July 1941, FDR created the post of 'Coordinator of Information' and appointed Donovan as its first holder.

After Pearl Harbour, the need for reliable intelligence was made abundantly clear. Donovan's department was renamed the Office of Strategic Services (OSS), which was the precursor to the CIA. Like the Special Operations Executive in the UK, the OSS was involved in everything from assassination attempts, agent running and information warfare.

The OSS had an entire branch dedicated to open-source intelligence. The OSS's research and analysis branch meticulously collected newspapers, journals, press clippings, radio broadcasts and reports from around the world, collecting, collating and harvesting information, whilst also hunting for photos and articles that may give away crucial intelligence about the enemy. It would only be a matter of time before the analogue collection and harvesting would move and embody the digital realm.

The OSS had pored over thousands of journals and newspapers, including obituaries in German regional newspapers, looking to collate data on important Nazis. Images of new battleships, bomb craters and aircraft were painstakingly collected and collated. When these were collectively assessed together, it allowed the OSS to assess and gain an insight into the state of its enemies. It is clear how the original OSS's activities are similar to today's OSINT investigations. Herald the new dawn of computers and from the OSS and SOE. It is impossible to argue the roots of open-source intelligence that stretches back almost a century. The method to collect, collate and check information in Donovan's day was clearly laborious; however, it served as an incredible benefit. Now, today, there are tens of billions of emails daily, with social media and groups of people in the millions, even billions of people using digital for everything from their grocery shopping, to ordering their new book, buying a house or booking a holiday. Digital information is certainly not in short supply.

It was after the Second World War that the discipline of OSINT became a major method for most governments and government agencies. Typically, OSINT capability was resourced by career librarians and researchers. The noun 'library' became an unfashionable term in the mid-2000s and few, if any, intelligence professionals sought to work in the field, when the sexy, secret world of agent-running and signals intelligence was available.

The Terrorist attacks of 9/11 increased the usefulness of OSINT, along with the launch of social media's Facebook in 2004 a few years later. Terrorist communications, voicemails and emails were captured and analysed using various technologies and OSINT. Photos, locations and messages were all harvested in an attempt to gain insights and prevent further attacks.

A poorly kept secret was the CIA's investment and support of Facebook in full knowledge that citizens of the world would gladly share their most intimate secrets and information on their very own social platform. The public had little idea just how, and who was collecting, collating and harvesting the information to enable major campaigns and drive behaviours by the masses.

In 2009, Iran was on the brink of a bottom-up 'Green Revolution'. Many of Iran's citizens, now much younger and keen to make their own decisions, were protesting against the regime. Millions of young Iranians used the Internet to coordinate activities, share content and encourage others to join their campaigns. The Internet was flooded with citizens' information about major political events, largely thanks to the combination of new smartphones, Internet connections and social media. Things were vastly different during the early weeks of this Iranian protest.

During this period, Internet use in Iran increased from 34 per cent of the population in 2008 to 48 per cent in 2009. This was a marked increase. Mobile phone usage and subscriptions increased from 59 per cent to 72 per cent of Iran's population. The BBC ran an article at the time titled 'Internet Brings Iran to Life', where it claimed a new form of 'citizen journalism' was thriving.

Individuals around the world, for the first time, could utilise social networks for intelligence and content and, in the process, write articles, forecasts and deliver insightful intelligence analysis. Whilst the protests in Iran were ultimately unsuccessful, the regime quickly reasserted control of the Internet.

It is not surprising that journalists, researchers and investigators led much of the development of OSINT as a discipline which is unequivocally a field that continues constantly to evolve and moves at light speed and in near real time. New tools and techniques are continuously being developed, honed and created almost daily. The worlds of academia and government have only more recently started to realise the enormous potential of this data when used for good. Individuals who may have previously been constrained by bureaucracy or poor IT can quickly become adept OSINT operators, and create insights, patterns and connections that were previously unknown.

So, now we know how OSINT originally started, where OSINT has got to, and what it should and can be used for. If we look at more recent examples of OSINT technology, it was unquestionably developed to aid security professionals to run checks across their Internet facing connections, be they websites, subdomains, servers or domain name servers (DNS)/content delivery network (CDN) providers. Once they identified any suboptimal positions due to oversight, or even negligence, they could address and remediate the positions.

To recap history a little, hypertext transfer protocol (HTTP) was superseded by hypertext transfer protocol secure (HTTPS), which was rolled out in 2018. Any website failing to use the latest and secure protocol would display a 'not secure' text in the address bar, which confirmed the lack of a secure connection. Furthermore, Google and other providers relegated non-HTTPS websites so that they were pushed down their SEO positions in an attempt (a) to protect website visitors, and (b) to encourage companies at least to take the basic steps to use the latest secure protocols. Cybercrime was running at an all-time and alarming rate and only a planet-scale change would make any marked difference.

It is an incredibly sad fact that companies need to be 'shamed' into ensuring that they take the very basic of security measures and here we are four years later and still there are millions of organisations, including governments, that do not adhere to the practice, leaving their organisation and website visitors open to cyberattacks.

Look at recent cyberattacks on CNA insurance, Travelex, AXA, JBS and Colonial. All these and thousands of others have suffered cyberattacks whilst maintaining 'not secure' websites. This not only flagged them up as being 'not secure' for the world to see in their website addresses, but also sent notifications of their cyberattack on websites displaying as 'not secure'. It is beyond reckless; it is nothing short of pathetic.

I have mentioned secure socket layer (SSL) tests throughout this book. SSL and transport layer security (TLS) are cryptographic protocols designed to provide communications security over a computer network. The protocol is widely used and applications such as email, instant messaging, and Voice over Internet Protocol (VOIP) use it extensively.

One of the very first OSINT security tests to run is typically a Qualys SSL Labs test that provides a great deal of information on the status of several things, including the digital certificate itself, protocol support, key exchange, and cipher strength. SSL Lab tests, as with all OSINT technology, should ideally be A rated and SSL quickly identifies, and confirms, or otherwise, secure communication over a network. SSL Labs is one of the most well-known and used OSINT technologies available. It begs the question then why so many companies do not get this basic OSINT check right, which leaves their website displaying as 'not secure', as we witnessed across many Ukraine government websites. This confirmed that, quite possibly since 2018, nobody had upgraded and simply set the SSL annual renewal to auto renew, ensuring the website remains 'not secure' year after year. As mentioned elsewhere in this book, only after informing www.mfa.gov.ua of their 'not secure' displaying website did they finally renew the correct digital certificate on 16 March, some eight weeks later. As a footnote, a cybercriminal can not only gain access to a 'not secure' website but can do so in the time you take to read this chapter, often quicker.

It is at this point we frequently confirm that an SSL security test taken in isolation is quite worthless as it only represents around 10 per cent of the entire security element a website needs to have, and to be able to demonstrate to avoid making it, and the company exposed and vulnerable to being exploited. Let me give you an example. Let us assume that the SSL test shows up as A+, all four elements are green and looking great as the example below shows. Any security professional would be very happy with this SSL security test and scan. However, as mentioned, one should *never* consider their job as a security professional of securing the company's websites or servers as being secure simply on this result on its own.

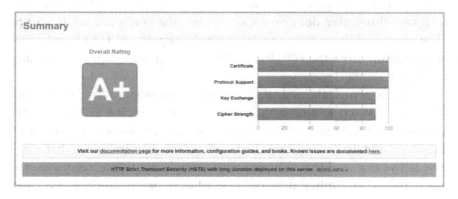

Armed with the fact that the above SSL security test is A+ rated, the next thing they should look at are the HTTP headers and configuration. This is the single largest failure point we continually witness. The below is the same website and same company who, for legal reasons, shall remain nameless at this time. As we can see, there are many red Xs. Each red X represents major exposed vulnerabilities, but how can this alert a would-be cybercriminal without going through a full set of OSINT scans? Just as importantly, how can a security professional sign off the company's Internet security position without undertaking full security tests? They simply cannot and security becomes an assumption and not evidence.

Content Security Policy	✗	-25	Content Security Policy (CSP) header not implemented
Cookies	✗	-40	Session cookie set without using the Secure flag or set over HTTP
Cross-origin Resource Sharing	✓	0	Content is not visible via cross-origin resource sharing (CORS) files or headers
HTTP Public Key Pinning	—	0	HTTP Public Key Pinning (HPKP) header not implemented (optional)
HTTP Strict Transport Security	✗	-20	HTTP Strict Transport Security (HSTS) header not implemented
Redirection	✗	-20	Does not redirect to an HTTPS site
Referrer Policy	—	0	Referrer-Policy header not implemented (optional)
Subresource Integrity	✗	-5	Subresource Integrity (SRI) not implemented, but all external scripts are loaded over HTTPS
X-Content-Type-Options	✗	-5	X-Content-Type-Options header not implemented
X-Frame-Options	✓	0	X-Frame-Options (XFO) header set to SAMEORIGIN or DENY
X-XSS-Protection	✗	-10	X-XSS-Protection header not implemented

If we look at the above OSINT scan, not only does it clearly show a sub-optimal security position, but if we look at line 6, it says, 'does not redirect to HTTPS site'. In other words, no matter what digital certificate the SSL scan says this server does or does not have, the configuration is set up incorrectly and the website is relying on the deprecated HTTP and so is *not* benefiting from the HTTPS, the latest and greatest digital certificate and its A+ rating.

In simple terms, the website these two screenshots relate to will be showing a 'not secure' text in the uniform resource locator (URL) website address bar. It will therefore be alerting every casual visitor or cybercriminal on reconnaissance in their bedroom, office or warehouse, that they have a 'live one' and that the company is simply not taking security seriously. The cybercriminal does not care what errors on configuration are made or what security headers are missing. They will simply confirm to the attack launch team they are good to launch an attack and that that will get an easy passage.

What the company above inadvertently, or otherwise, has confirmed in two simple OSINT scans is that it is doing some, but not all, security processes and that those processes are assumed to be correct, unchecked and left for another 12 months for a further period as insecure. This is exactly as the Lloyd's CISO declared and was falling foul of in addition to their DNS CNAME and others being insecure. He was busy waving his SSL A rated scan, declaring Lloyd's was secure, all the while the website was misconfigured.

OSINT technology was, as this chapter has clearly demonstrated, set up to enable the so-called good guys to ensure and check their work (quality control) and the security of the company paying their salaries. Sadly, as this single example shows, a cybercriminal can easily and, often within minutes, identify and then launch attacks on insecure websites, servers, DNS and companies using the very same OSINT technology that the good guys are using supposedly to check they are secure.

The situation is not dissimilar to when HTTP was superseded by HTTPS. It was to enforce improved security for the masses; however, due to oversight, resource constraints, incompetence or even negligence, the adoption of HTTPS was not universally adopted and that made companies' websites that did not upgrade 'not secure' and display the same for the world to see. Cybercriminals rarely need an invite. Perversely, it made companies easily identifiable and easy targets. I suggest that 2018 will go down as the year target practice and reconnaissance of insecure and 'not secure' companies was gifted to the cybercriminal world.

Truth be told, the world is losing billions of dollars every day because companies are first making themselves easy targets by *not* doing the basics. Their actions, or lack thereof, not only make them an easily identified target, but also a target that can be easily exploited using any of dozens and dozens of offensive website and server techniques—techniques that were originally designed developed, and perfected by government agencies over recent decades.

This chapter has only covered a tiny portion of the extensive range of OSINT, as it is constantly expanding. However, let me confirm one thing. No matter what endpoint protection, anti-virus, phishing monitoring or other network protection a company thinks it has, if the company's DNS or public key infrastructure is sub-optimal, or compromised, every dollar spent on security and security resource is futile and negated, as nobody, apart from cybercriminals, is looking and the insecure position of basic security will go totally unnoticed until the attack surfaces. Then it is simply too late and it is damage limitation and a matter of pulling the 'sophisticated' card out.

CHAPTER 7

Digital Perimeter Defences

O NE OF THE BEST ways to explain the implications of security errors within the technologies we have now covered in this book is my perimeter defence theory.

All-around defence or perimeter defence is a type of defensive fighting position intended to give military units the ability to repel attacks from any direction. The positioning of the outer defensive fighting positions of a unit is typically circular or triangular in form, from a bird's-eye view.

Perimeter defence is a tried and tested military methodology and position, and has been practised almost as long as wars have been around. You will also be familiar with the term 'taking the high ground'. In the case of warfare, it is to take an elevated terrain or position, which is useful in combat. The military importance of the high ground has been acknowledged for over 2,000 years and records from China and other eastern dynastic cultures, who frequently engaged in territorial/power struggles.

In more recent years, taking the high ground was incorporated and seen as advantageous, which is why fortresses and castles are typically built higher than the surrounding areas and included high perimeter walls which provided protection and were used to fire down upon one's enemies.

John Wycliffe so eloquently said in 1382: 'No thing vndir the sunne is newe', which, when translated to modern English, translates to: 'There is nothing new under the sun', the meaning of which is that there is nothing new under the sun, everything has existed before.

DOI: 10.1201/9781003323273-9

Perimeter defence is exactly that, nothing new and something that has been tried and tested. It is a must for today's modern warfare, and that must include cyber warfare.

Let us consider a modern-day equivalent of 'circling the wagons'. Let's use an example I shared with the head of the Ministry of Defence (MOD) here in the UK and its Academy that suffered a digital intrusion in March 2021. The academy has high wired perimeter defences that run around the entire perimeter. The wired fencing runs unbroken and continuously around the entire perimeter, breaking only at the access point. This 'access' is heavily guarded by armed soldiers with extremely strict and stringent instructions. The MOD Academy trains over 28,000 senior forces personnel each year.

The MOD Academy has 24-hour a day security, alarms and oversight with cameras and every security measure one might expect. There is some very sensitive information being discussed and shared within the confines of the perimeter. So, is the perimeter secure then? Well, to an extent it is, on a physical level; however, on a digital level, apparently it was not. We believe—indeed, we know—that nobody gained illegal access to the academy under the cover of darkness or clandestinely plugged in a USB stick, that is so National Security Agency (NSA) of 20 years ago. Well, that did actually happen when USB sticks were found in the NSA carparks and inquisitive NSA operatives wanted to check what was on the stick. They went into their office and plugged the USB stick in, not realising, or indeed thinking, the stick might contain malware, which it did.

So, putting the USB theory aside, what other options for infiltrating the MOD Academy's secure perimeter is there? Well, let us think about how the MOD academy accesses the Internet. The entire academy is wired with the latest and greatest cabling, copper and fibre optic, no doubt a mix of the two, it really does not matter for this example. Somewhere under the perimeter of the MOD Academy these cables run to enable power and Internet connectivity in the form of telephone cables supplied by one of many companies, BT, Vodafone, Virgin or Huawei. Sorry, I could help myself, not Huawei, or at least hopefully not: stranger, ridiculous issues have occurred.

One end of the cable goes into a wall socket or similar to enable a user to plug in local servers and devices that feed local PCs and laptops. Add routers and possibly even WIFIs that might use virtual private networks (VPNs) and so on. The other end may go into a device, third-party provider and outsourced contracts to Serco, Fujitsu or similar for such services.

So far so good. We know where the cables go, where they are at each end, and who is responsible for which part, or so we think. As part of the contracts, the website and email servers will be using an Internet service provider (ISP) who, in turn, will use a domain name system (DNS) provider and who, in turn, may also be providing content delivery network (CDN) or using another supplier.

Let us recap the schematic for a moment. We have moved from a highly secure, perimeter confined, armed guarded MOD base, through some tiny cables, copper or fibre, and through several providers that provide website and emails, ISP, DNS and CDN. Rarely will all these be the same company, but several.

If we consider company A provides website and email management, company B is an ISP provider, company C provides the DNS and, finally, company D provides CDN services. So, we have the MOD Academy and possibly four separate companies providing services that ultimately allow a user within the academy and barracks to use the Internet and send or receive an email. That is a large number of points of failure to consider and ensure all security is checked both upon contract as part of the due diligence (DD) process, and on an ongoing basis. Advanced persistent threats (APTs) are well known and hundreds, even thousands of attacks will occur daily on such targets as the MOD.

Let us assume company A has first-class security and also has excellent controls, management and governance of its DNS positions and, in doing so, does *not* add or detract from the security position of the MOD Academy.

Let us assume that company B also has first class security and also manages its DNS positions and by doing so, also does *not* compromise the MOD's security position.

Company C as a DNS provider knows exactly what it is doing in the DNS space so has all its eggs in a row and, as such, takes basic security and discipline very seriously. It comes easy for the company. Some members of the company are actually former MOD Academy attendees: keep it in the family, so to speak. Company C does *not* detract or compromise the MOD Academy's security.

Company D has a great reputation and provides services to numerous other government entities. However, DD was 'glossed over' and neither sought nor seen as being required. It was simply a signing of a contract after a 'faut au compli' beauty parade that may or may not have taken place, costs are agreed upon and contracts are duly signed. Drinks all round then.

Now consider an alternative, and one that we believe, in fact, we know occurred. What if company A does *not* have first class security and is actually already exposed and can be easily compromised. Company A looks after the websites and emails. Company B also has issues, and its security is far from ideal, so much so that it has unknowingly had malware and code injected two years ago by perpetrators who are in full knowledge that the 'targeted' company supplies services to the MOD Academy. Company C, even though a DNS company, has been rather remiss and allowed a number of its critical servers to be compromised due to misconfigured PKI issues and flawed auto-renewed digital certificates, which means that the error is replicated annually, unknowingly and thus maintains the insecure position year on year.

Finally, company D is the CDN and provides services for other government entities and is of the highest security clearance. However, Company D too has configuration errors of its own DNS, which now also totally compromises the MOD Academy due to insecure DNS records, including its DNS zone. In other words, backdoors abound at companies A, B, C and D and nobody is either looking or checking, which results in a cyberattack. Once again symptoms are addressed, tens of millions of pounds are spent and wasted on replacing software and hardware that is then plugged back in and connecting to the Internet via the same insecure providers, and the cause, once again, is ignored. This is completely reckless and is exactly what is happening constantly.

Each and every one of these providers is confident it is secure and has multi-million-pound contracts. However, not one of them is checking its own perimeter defences, which in turn nullifies the perimeter of, in this case, the MOD Academy.

Furthermore, as I demonstrated to the former head of the MOD Academy, the Academy too does *not* look at its digital perimeter, which leaves it totally exposed to digital infiltration and intrusion, which is exactly what happened. At the time, one of the third-party suppliers took the flak for the security issue and exposure. However, our research shows that it could have been any one of the companies and, in addition, the MOD Academy itself. In other words, although I fully respect the knowledge of kinetic warfare and warfare strategies, I am left totally unimpressed with the digital security of this government organisation which was, during the digital infiltration, totally exposed to numerous DNS and PKI issues and still is to this day, as are the MOD suppliers and partners. This is NOT security by design, but insecurity by default.

As this book has continually stated and shown, the basics of digital security are, and always have been, domain name systems (DNS) and public key infrastructure (PKI) and were accepted as the global gold standard in 1986 and then again around 1995. A push towards open source, artificial intelligence (AI) and many other such technologies has made the vast majority of people relaxed, even lazy and foolishly continually ignoring the basics. This has led to a plethora of insecure websites and email servers, DNS, PKI and CDNs. Cybercriminals, or cyber soldiers, do *not* need to work hard; they simply need to identify human oversight and basic security errors to exploit. These they find in the digital world facing and connected to the Internet in droves, many millions of times over.

Defence in depth is another military term that acknowledges the first layer, as well as other layers of defence, that, although critical, may delay rather than completely prevent intrusion by an attacker. Nowhere will you ever see defence in depth suggesting the first layer of defence be missed or made simple to exploit. Yet in the digital world, when errors are made and, in essence, completely removing the first layer, the perimeter of defence, the layer where the organisations' Internet facing and connected security is missed due to oversight, complacency, or ignorance is that critical juncture, it can then be open season and the loss of command and control.

By having a resilient first line of defence, it greatly reduces and deflects efforts to gain further access. Remember in cases like Stuxnet and SolarWinds, once access is made through the first layer, via DNS or PKI errors and poor controls, it is almost certain that access to all areas will be easy. In truth, such access can become like a backstage pass to your favourite band. If access is gained to a website or email server, it is again almost certainly game over as then, to use another military term, the enemy is inside the perimeter and masquerading as one of their own. Any attacker that meets a position, digital or otherwise, knowing there is defence in depth, knows it is not a single access point or blow to achieve the win. Defence in depth relies upon the fact that an attack loses momentum over time or must penetrate several, resilient layers. If it is just one, it is much simpler.

Sub-domain takeovers, for example, as happened at SolarWinds, can be enabled through expired hosting services or DNS misconfigurations. Once attackers have privileges on the system after taking over the sub-domain, they can upload files, create databases, monitor data traffic and clone the main website. Worse, it is not possible to easily detect that the sub-domain has been hijacked, leaving the enterprise's system vulnerable to many different types of attacks. It was poorly managed and lacked controls in the first place.

A conventional defence strategy might concentrate all military resources on the front line, which if breached by an attacker would leave the remaining forces in danger of being outflanked and then surrounded, leaving supply lines, communications and command vulnerable. This is exactly what happens when the digital front line is breached due to errors or basic security is overlooked, even ignored.

However, once an attacker losses momentum or is forced to attack on numerous fronts, defensive counterattacks can be mounted. This is no different when applying cybersecurity to an organisation and this method is strongly recommended. Defence in depth in the digital realm is something every company should ensure. However, a word of warning, the company *must* ensure the first layer and that the Internet connectivity is secure, as failure to do so will typically and simply circumvent and negate all other forms of security. Honeypots are also a useful addition here. A honeypot is a network attached system set up as a decoy to lure cyberattackers and to detect, and deflect, even study hacking attempts.

We have researched over 1,000 organisations and, sadly, that number increases daily. All those that have suffered cyber and ransomware attacks and, in every case, be it Central Bank, SolarWinds, CNA insurance, JBS Foods, Mondelez, Okta or Gazprom, the discovery of sub-optimal basic security has been discovered across the board.

Cyber and ransomware attacks can arise from missing security headers, missing content security policy (CSP-) cross-site scripting (X-XSS) (listed as OWASPS No 3 exploited vulnerability), HTTP not directing to HTTPS, invalid digital certificates, or insecure DNS or CDN positions not being maintained, and so on. It is not rocket science and takes discipline and knowledge.

A good friend of mine stated recently that those with ultimate responsibility and accountability cannot outsource either. They can only outsource some accountability by delegating authority. When you use a DNS/CDN provider, you are outsourcing authority and accountability; you are *not* outsourcing responsibility, as that will always remain with the parent company.

We have made it all the easier simply to identify organisations that have dropped their guard by showing their websites as 'not secure' since 2018 in the address bar and by using open-source intelligence (OSINT) to identify companies that have PKI or DNS issues. As Dan Kaminsky stated over

10 years ago, people aim to compromise websites and emails. Which part of that statement is hard to understand and then to ensure that they are secure and enjoy proper security controls and management?

In the words of the Eagles' song *Lying Eyes*: 'Did she get tired or did she just get lazy? She's so far gone she feels just like a fool.'

Sadly, the last two generations of humanity have shuffled between knowing, not knowing, doing and not doing. This has created something of a highly toxic cocktail that is unpalatable, weaponised, and very, very dangerous.

We have witnessed leaders like Dan Kaminsky and Paul Vixie who actually make a stand for security, whilst governments might simply prefer them to go away and be silent. We have personally witnessed being marginalised for calling out Chinese and Russian digital certificates with lengthy validity and administration privileges within critical infrastructure (CI) and big 4's. Maybe it is time to publish that critical infrastructure report now. If you lie down with dogs. . .

To put this chapter in some sort of context, currently the world's connections to the Internet are woefully insecure at best and across a massive percentage of organisations and the billion plus websites, let alone the named servers and millions of others. Like dominos, DNS, when working well, just like border gateway protocol (BGP) works really well, get it wrong and it goes wrong on a potentially global basis very rapidly. We have witnessed this numerous times across the world. We love being connected but neglect security at literally every turn.

Stuxnet was turned against US banks and energy, WannaCry crippled the National Health Service (NHS) in the UK, and malware attacks in Ukraine as part of the overall cyberwar has compounded, dare I say, cyberwar, in this instance, played a pre-emptive and then ongoing cameo role that is supporting the kinetic fuelled the War Machine that Russia commenced nine months ago.

III

Examples of Previous Attacks
and Insecurities

CHAPTER 8

US Government Security Failings

I N THE MID-1990S, WITH the continued explosion of personal computers, public key infrastructure (PKI) was globally adopted. PKI was made up of digital certificates and keys issued by certificate authorities (CAs).

In the simplest of explanations, digital certificates and keys are electronic credentials that provide authentication and validation of users and devices. They also play a vital part in encryption and decryption. Think of a digital certificate as an electronic passport. Digital certificates can be simply updated enabling stronger ciphers (codes) and can provide encryption for those transmitting and those receiving communications, instructions, payments and so on. It is important to note, however, that these digital certificates need managing and replacing, typically annually, sometimes more frequently. When certificates become invalid, and are not replaced, security becomes an issue.

PKI can use stronger, more complex digital certificates and keys, depending on the requirement, all the way to post-quantum computing and be rotated accordingly. Equally, certificates are deprecated and revoked when found to be too weak or when used illegally. These must be replaced and upgraded to ensure security or risk becoming insecure and exposed to being exploited. These vulnerabilities will, eventually, be hacked. The Optus cyberattack in October 2022 was due to access being achieved via an exposed API. Our research that was shared with Optus and the Chief Commissioner of Australia's Federal Police showed one particular API Optus subdomain was using, and had

DOI: 10.1201/9781003323273-11

been using for some time, a Revoked digital certificate. This made the website 'not secure' and easily exploitable.

Unlike the Enigma and Lorenz machines of the Second World War, modern computers do not need to be completely swapped out; their security can be simply managed by upgrading the digital certificates and keys. You may be familiar with 'patch Tuesday', the numerous common vulnerabilities and exposures (CVEs), and the certificate revocation list (CRL), which is a list of certificates found to have been used for nefarious purposes and requiring revoking, replacing and upgrading. This has become a discipline that must be adhered to and not neglected. It is also a major area used by cybercriminals to identify and gain access to networks.

Everything was going swimmingly from the start of PKI until, unfortunately, soon thereafter, certain governments developed insatiable appetites to gain inside visibility just as they did with DNS. Never was this more so post 9/11, to enable them to eavesdrop digitally on suspected terrorists. One program (Stellarwind) was rolled out with the assistance of numerous, let us call them, 'incentivised' tech giants and global telecommunication companies. The program was simple and allowed backdoors to be planted here, there and everywhere, in any, and every company, organisation, even other governments across all regions, by using clandestine plants and backdoors.

A particular favourite was backdoors using compromised digital certificates, often with the capability of providing full administration access and controls. This was often without the knowledge or consent of the organisation. Put simply, who would know if an enterprise, containing millions of certificates contained a few rogue certificates with full privileges and access to contact the mothership, whomever and wherever that was. . .

The CIA took this a step further by secretly owning the Swiss encryption companies Crypto AG and OMNISEC. Both provided cryptography machines to no less than 120 countries, including allies and, of course, all the machines were constructed with certain CIA backdoors built in. Digital eavesdropping at government level has not changed since the Cold War and before; the methods simply evolved to become digital.

These campaigns received government consent initially by President Bush, then President Obama under the auspices of defending the US and wider world against terrorism. It was not long before the temptation to use the method of digital certificates was simply too intoxicating, not just to eavesdrop for intelligence but also to use the same method for offensive purposes, which would go on to cause collateral damage.

There is a fine line between defensive and offensive operations and both can frequently be used for either. Shortly afterwards, Project Aurora was undertaken, the first use of 'bytes' for offensive purposes and not long after around 2007, Stuxnet was on the cyber warfare drawing board.

Project Aurora saw code injected to override the control system of a huge diesel machine's normal running cycle. This machine would usually be found providing megawatts for the US national grid and was literally blown up simply by using code to speed up and slow it down, causing the machine and the harmonics to fail.

This effectively destroyed the machine and became the basis for Flame, Duqu and then Stuxnet.

Cryptography over the years has failed due to the fact if a person can create it, it is only a matter of time before someone else can break it. The situation is massively expedited due to PKI compromises globally. No longer does an adversary need to decrypt the code; he simply needs to look like he is part of the internal PKI and gain access via stolen, fake, and compromised certificates and encrypted keys. Or via websites that are only using hypertext transfer protocol (HTTP), which since 2018 means the website lacks authentication, data integrity and data in transit is in plaintext, or unencrypted as it is meant to be.

Pandora's box was open to the ease of gaining full insight and even taking over command and control (C2), whilst everything looked normal. It was simply a matter of time before adversaries managed to gain the same capability using the same methods, modus operandi (MO), and techniques. Training and certification in offensive website capabilities is big business and agencies and cybercriminals look for such professional certifications as a prerequisite when recruiting.

THE US ELECTIONS AND CRITICAL INFRASTRUCTURE

In May 2020, our research team was asked to run passive scans on a number of US and Canadian government and country domains. This included state-run Internet-facing sites and servers. These sites are also connected for such things as emergency COVID-19 funding and electronic voting. They also collect, collate and share personal identifiable information (PII). If the site is 'not secure', such information—with the right tools and expertise—is easily accessible.

There are a number of regulatory bodies, the National Institute of Standards and Technology (NIST), the International Organization for Standardization (ISO), and several other governing bodies whose minimum recommendations are simply not being met. Let us not forget: these are government domains. Furthermore, not only are their standards not being met, they are not meeting them themselves.

In simple terms, what was discovered at several sites clearly evidenced systemic issues that, if left unchecked and not remediated, could enable digital intrusion and infiltration, traversing and lateral movement across these and other connected domains. Exfiltration of data and ultimately taking over command and control gaining access and changing passwords, even the ability to lock users out. Think of it like this: you have left your house wide open for weeks, months, even years. The keys and all treasured possessions are left on the table and a thief can simply stroll in, start taking up residence and change all the locks.

These sites tell a tale of up to a decade of non-compliance with basic security, sometimes even more. Poor management, and negligence, as well as the use of SHA-1 certificates that were deprecated as far back as 2011 are frequently found at government websites. SHA-1 certificates were deprecated due to ease of being successfully attacked and broken. Ironically, the National Security Agency (NSA) was hacked in 2012 via a SHA-1 certificate. Do not forget, if, as in this case, a root certificate is untrusted, in simple terms the access and lateral movement by an adversary enables controls and privileges, as well as access to all PII, which can be easily accessed and used. Such information includes names, addresses, driving licences, social information, ages; in short, everything to cause chaos and digital identity theft. Privacy laws are there to protect the public.

In March and April 2020, the German government was stung in a cybersquatting campaign and over a two-week period paid out €100 million to COVID-19 funding support for individuals. The German government inadvertently paid cybercriminals who had captured and harvested the PII data of Real Claimants. The criminals had duplicated and stood up an Evil Twin website the German government had to support Small Business and Self Employed. Then the criminals used the real data to claim financial support by the government.

The criminals had gathered the right PII information and had the right credentials. In the government's rush to support organisations and to make COVID-19 payments to those people that required it, they did not exercise enough diligence or caution. They paid the money, but instead of paying the legitimate claimants, they paid the cybercriminals who had stolen the credentials and used these stolen identities on an industrial scale for just two weeks. It was only when the complaints were amassing from non-receipt of funds by the real claimants that checks were made.

Similar situations are possible everywhere and already taking place. A US Internal Revenue Service (IRS) scheme is still paying out to the wrong people years after the event due to a comparable situation. What does this mean to the government, the digital electoral system, and the PII they collect when uncontrolled and unmanaged?

Put simply, it makes all the above incredibly vulnerable and susceptible to breaches and data theft, leaving organisations and governments totally exposed to digital intrusion. The electoral data can unequivocally be tampered with, the information can be used, sold and manipulated by other 'interested parties', including nation states. The government would clearly fall foul of all regulations on privacy—in short, it would be a complete mess—a major car crash in the making on a potentially countrywide, or even global, scale. Think how this could impact a war effort and disrupt a military operation.

Furthermore, if one were to think like a hacker (and not as an upstanding citizen just for a moment) and wanted to gain access to critical information including critical infrastructure, electoral voting sites or even the IRS site, what route would the hacker take? Clearly, the route of least resistance and those simple routes are everywhere and typically blamed on nation states or 'sophisticated' attacks. Exposed positions are simply exploited.

Remember the house above, doors left open, keys and possessions on the table, zero resistance. These 'not secure' websites are the path of least resistance and enable, through traversing, digital trust and privileges, not only moving around a website, but all associated websites. Full digital trust enables such outcomes with little no resistance. The SolarWinds cyberattack is a case in point of exactly this type of sequence of events which resulted in 18,000 subsequent cyberattacks including the US government and Treasury.

Alaska was one of those we were asked to scan. The Alaska Division of Elections website declares: 'Our mission is to ensure public confidence in the electoral process by administering voter registration and elections with the highest level of professional standards, integrity, security, accuracy and fairness.'

On 29 May 2020, we discovered, through routine intelligence, that the website and web server hosting the site for the Alaska Division of Elections was highly vulnerable to cyberattacks, which could result in the Alaskan State losing command and control of its electoral system, exposing personally identifiable information and bringing the total security of the US voting system into question. The domain clearly showed that it was 'not secure'. There were some 23 major vulnerabilities and many common vulnerabilities and exposures (CVEs) dating back all the way to 2010. These should have been changed immediately but were left in place for over a decade. The Alaskan government has now suffered at least four separate cyberattacks from voting to the court and judicial system.

Alaska is just one of several US states we investigated, and many have similar security issues that urgently require attention. Even the previous President of the United States, Donald Trump, suffered a website cyberattack prior to the elections. When we researched, we discovered several 'not secure' Donald Trump websites, which no doubt were manipulated to gain access.

There are profoundly serious implications to such findings, as recently also happened to Archer—the UK's supercomputer in Edinburgh. Only weeks before Archer's cyberattack, the homepage's digital certificate had expired, making the website 'not secure' and confirming a lack of PKI controls and management. Archer was then shortly thereafter the victim of a cyberattack. Archer worked on clinical research for universities and pharmaceutical organisations which had spent billions of dollars on research and collecting and collating data, which was exfiltrated with the yet to be proven theft by China due to invaluable research including the critical data on COVID-19. The total cost of this research runs into billions.

As John F. Kennedy said: 'There are risks and costs to action. But they are far less than the long-range risks of comfortable inaction.'

The research work, passive scanning and experiences we have briefly touched upon here show that either through a lack of knowledge, assumptions, inability, ignorance or gross negligence, PKI and websites are like Swiss cheese—full of holes. None of these examples, and there are thousands more, including government, state-run financially critical and digital voting sites can provide the assurances to the public on privacy, whilst being in complete contravention of all guidelines. The rules governing such data collection and management, and the apparent challenge to do so securely, is evidence of systemic issues that undermine all elections and local infrastructure, privacy and security.

In addition to this, the Federal Bureau of Investigation (FBI) recently warned the US government facilities sector (GFS) and their partners of an increase in offensive cyberattacks on local government agencies that resulted in disruption of services and risks to the public, let alone the financial implications. The FBI did *not* tell them they would suffer these attacks by the very same means they, the FBI, had used for decades but failed to tell anyone of the security oversights.

It was only late last year that the FBI itself fell foul of website and email server attacks. The attacks saw the distribution of 100,000 FBI cyberwarning attacks with malicious content that were sent by cybercriminals who had taken over command and control of FBI servers due to the FBI lacking basic security controls. In other words, the techniques and tactics the FBI uses itself, was used against it. It is easy to see the FBI's calls for action and advice being somewhat questioned.

In response to the publication, I responded with the following message: what the FBI really should do is to arm these organisations with the ability to protect themselves by educating them to ensure that fundamental and basic security measures are in place as opposed to leaving their websites and servers exposed and insecure. That would be the single biggest gift the FBI could ever give these guys.

The sentiment is indeed, as we say, bang on the money, or on point. The FBI itself got caught out because it overlooked, ignored and lacked control of basic security that it abused and that is domain name system (DNS) and public key infrastructure (PKI). Both provide the very foundation of *all* security.

The NSA and the FBI, among many other agencies once under the stewardship of Jim Gosler, Michael Hayden and many others, have spent decades abusing the very security and foundations developed to provide that security and have simply fallen foul themselves of the same basic security errors and negligence that provided them with unrestricted access. However, with so much sensitive information and continued insecurity, surely this must be classed as gross negligence?

As has been confirmed, the FBI was hacked several months ago, and the screenshot taken below from 2 April 2022 shows that http://fbi.gov.cdn .cloudflare.net as being 'not secure'. This is the FBI.gov DNS CNAME. It should always resolve and never be 'not secure'.

▲ Not secure | http://fbi.gov.cdn.cloudflare.net

The uniform resource locator (URL) http://fbi.gov.cdn.cloudlfare.net is the FBI's DNS record canonical name (CNAME) and, due to a misconfiguration by Cloudflare, the http version is not redirecting to the secure hypertext transfer protocol secure (HTTPS) version, which leaves the FBI exposed and exploitable to many cyberattacks including Man-in-The-Middle (MiTM) attacks and email server access. This is exactly what the FBI suffered only months ago and declared it had resolved the error. The FBI may have discovered and fixed 'an' error, but clearly not this error, which the above evidence shows.

We have previously assisted the FBI and played our part. We are not US citizens, but citizens of the world, and do not want our way of life to be radically changed by allowing such foolish errors, ransomware and cyberattacks. We barely got a thank you and have shared the above information with the Cybersecurity and Infrastructure Security Agency (CISA), the FBI and many other senior US government officials. The continued lack of knowledge and ignorance is astounding, as can be seen by simply leaving the situation exposed.

What makes it all the more maddening is the White House, the NSA, the FBI and the CISA have all very recently released papers, documents, and, in the last 12 months, even videos (CISA) on the criticality of PKI and domain name systems (DNSs), so many times it is hard to keep count. In the latest White House paper released only one week after Ukraine cyberwar attacks started and titled, 'Moving the US government to a Zero Trust Model', the paper cited HTTP and HTTPS 132 times and DNS 47 times. As stated, this paper was released on 26 January 2022, just a week after the world's first ever cyberwar on Ukraine. Yet, as we continually evidence, the US government and Intelligence Community themselves typically maintain poor basic security controls and measures, which can and are then used to facilitate digital access in the form of either web or email server attacks. The above FBI 100,000 nefarious emails are a case in point.

With the cyberwar raging alongside ever-increasing global ransomware and cyberattacks and kinetic warfare, it is all too confusing to understand if we are simply surrounded by complete incompetence and negligence or if there is a higher power in charge coordinating the situation with an end game plan?

With cyberattacks at the highest level ever in the history of humanity, the cost of living at the highest in the history of humanity, a war in Europe for the first time in nearly 80 years, and cyber security firms unable to do anything other than blame sophisticated attacks whilst maintaining their own insecure positions, it is a job to see how this will end any other way than terribly badly. Dick Turpin at least had the decency to wear a mask!

We live in a very confusing and controlling time. We are all encouraged, in fact forced to do our banking online (so many bank premises are closing) and to become a cashless society. Do not even get me started on digital currency and the appalling insecurity and theft. We are required to order our food and clothes online whilst stores continue to close, thus vastly reducing their expenditure and overheads. Just count the closed shops in your local high street and see the differences and options online and look at the cookies, manipulated backdoor DNS and the data capture and monetisation. What shops are left are now encouraged to take emails as part of digital capture to start creating a digital you to start profiling for later use and even monetising. We are graded by numerous metrics and nudge theory (very much alive and kicking) and 'human action' will determine your group, age, voting and buying habits through controlled social media and numerous algorithms.

That is all well and good and, for convenience, the vast majority of people in the world think everything is fine. The likes of Jeff Bezos, Mark Zuckerberg and Jack Ma of the world realised that 'products and services' will always be in demand, and it is in their distribution that great wealth will be created. The only challenge each one of these organisations considered seriously is that they are also responsible for the security of the data, your data and the billions of customers they distribute to. In fact, after starting them it was not long before they all realised the new 'gold' was digital information and to monetise the data was a business, and an incredibly lucrative one all on its own.

Sadly, people, that is billions of people all around the world are not overly concerned about privacy, or digital trust. They are very happy to share all their details, intimate or otherwise, for free on social media platforms, or get cheaper products (limited stock and overheads). It may only hit them sometime later when they learn the hard way that their data has been sold, compromised or used for nefarious reasons and, just like the earlier chapter in this book, consider the symptom, and never the cause. Each one of the above companies, Facebook, Amazon and Alibaba are failing miserably, failing that is to provide basic security and protection for their users.

On each of their websites they may well tick many 'required' boxes and even have a perfectly and carefully written privacy notice of how they take the security of your data seriously; however, what they fail to tell their users is that the data makes them shed loads of money, lots, and lots of it. The privacy statement also fails, along with the security teams' oversight and negligence, and they all do *not* have basic security of the critical DNS and PKI under control and as such, no matter what they do, or do not do with your data to monetise it, they are, due to their basic security negligence, wide open to suffer digital infiltration and you, and your plain text data they have stored on you and billions of others, can be exfiltrated and used as the perpetrators wish, as has been done so, no doubt, on several occasions.

CHAPTER 9

UK Government Security Failings

DRESS REHERSALS ON THE MOD

In January 2022, just days before the cyberwar attack by Russia on Ukraine, a previous cyberattack on the UK's Ministry of Defence (MOD) Academy was formally disclosed and confirmed that it had caused 'significant' damage, which Edward Stringer, a recently retired high-ranking officer, revealed to SKY TV. Air Marshal Edward Stringer, who left the armed forces in August 2021, told *Sky News* about the attack, which had been discovered in March 2021, and which meant the MOD Academy was forced to address the cyberattack and rebuild its network.

Edward Stringer said he did not know if criminals, or hostile states, such as China, Russia, Iran or North Korea, were responsible, but the damage had yet to be fully rectified months later, Sky reported. Stringer also said: 'It could be any of those or it could just be someone trying to find a vulnerability for a ransomware attack that was just a genuine criminal organisation.'

He added: 'There were costs to... operational output. There were opportunity costs in what MOD staff could have been doing when, instead, they were having to repair the damage. And what could we be spending the money on that we have had to bring forward to rebuild the network? There are no bodies in the streets but there has still been some damage done.'

Sky News reported that no sensitive information was stored on the academy's network.

DOI: 10.1201/9781003323273-12

The MOD Academy is based in Shrivenham, Oxfordshire, and teaches around 28,000 military personnel, diplomats and civil servants a year. It had been forced to move online due to the COVID-19 pandemic.

In his interview with Sky, the first since he left the military, Stringer said 'unusual activity' was first discovered by contractors working for out-sourcing company Serco and 'alarm bells' started ringing.

He told the outlet there were 'external agents on our network who looked like they were there for what looked pretty quickly like nefarious reasons'. Stringer said the attack was not successful and, while the hackers may have been using the academy as a 'backdoor' to other MOD systems, there were no breaches beyond the school.

Stringer—who was also director general of joint force development and led the military thinking about how it would adapt to the future of warfare—said the attack fell within a so-called grey zone of harm, which falls below the threshold of war, according to *Sky News*.

I immediately contacted Edward Stringer and swapped emails with him within hours of this revelation and arranged to meet with him in London. There was much Edward Stringer was unaware of within the cyber realm, even as a military expert. Edward was new to cybersecurity, and with the world's first cyberwar looming, now was a perfect time to share our information and knowledge.

We initially had a phone call, which was followed by a lengthy meeting in London. In the phone call at 18:00 on 3 January 2022, I covered general cyber perimeter security, including public key infrastructure (PKI) and domain name system (DNS) issues. I had already looked at the security position of www.da.mod.uk and confirmed it was insecure, along with several insecure DNS records including web facing (A), mail exchange (MX), nameserver (NS), start of authority (SOA) and text (TXT).

On 4 January 2022, I sent an email to Edward with an attached com-prehensive report we had prepared on the current state of security of www.da.mod.uk and attached subdomains. The report showed numerous security errors and was dated 2 January 2022, some nine months after the cyberattack upon the MOD Academy in March 2021.

The report showed one MOD sub-domain, acms.mod.uk, had an expired digital certificate, which had expired on Saturday 15 May 2021 at 12:00 Coordinated Universal Time (UTC), some 234 days prior to the actual scan. When one looks at IP 94.236.30.120 it is a live IP address with both Ports 80 and 443 open today. There are 22 domains associated with this single MOD sub-domain, with consequential security issues.

The report also provided evidence of the overall website configuration and showed a cyber rated index (CRI) of F and 15. The worst CRI is F and 0 so, although not the worst, it was certainly not the A and 100 one might want to see, or indeed expect to see where the MOD's key domains are concerned.

The issues ranged from a missing content security policy (CSP), no HTTP strict transport security (HSTS), sub-resource issues and several missing security headers with the Open Web Application Security Project (OWASP) confirming that cross-site scripting (X-XSS) being the third most used website exploit being amongst the missing headers.

The following week I met with Edward in London and discussed the report, and the challenges organisations were facing, including UK government organisations, as well as the MOD itself. Edward had previously pointed out that he no longer worked within the government or the MOD, which of course was fully appreciated.

I was aware that, although previously a high-ranking Royal Air Force officer, cyber security was not Edward's area of expertise, even though only months before he was in charge of the MOD Academy whilst in the middle of the cyberattack and was tasked with the repercussion and remediation programme. The information and steep learning curve Edward was forced to go through would only be as good as those around him and I was educating him to the nuances of the actual attack, the methods, tactics and what, if anything, was at risk.

On 2 January 2022, I was the first person actually to register and perform a DNS scan on www.da.mod.uk, which confirms that nobody else had checked. That included the MOD and the Academy themselves, let alone any third-party suppliers. Cybercrime can go upstream, as well as downstream. This revelation is far from ideal, as DNS attacks and even the White House paper was only weeks after our meeting, and just weeks before PKI and DNS security errors enabled and facilitated cyberwar attacks upon the Ukraine government. It also confirmed a lack of control and management in this critical area of basic security. I can confirm that, in addition to the insecure DNS records that were included in the original report dated 2 January 2022, the da.mod.uk zone was insecure, and as can be seen below, still was at the time of writing (25 March 2022).

da.mod.uk

(2022-03-02 08:53:13 UTC)

Description: da.mod.uk zone
Status: INSECURE

The above screenshot shows the da.mod.uk zone as being insecure and that means everything across the network and enterprise. It could *not* be any worse, any more exposed and any more insecure.

In my meeting with Edward, I tried to use the perimeter defence analogy discussed in another chapter to simplify my message.

As a reminder, if we take a perimeter, in military terms, one must ensure that the perimeter is secure and that any access points are guarded appropriately, not every now and again, but full time. Invariably, everything is secure within the perimeter. The controls and management inside the perimeter is, as one might expect, secure.

When one connects to the Internet, certain exposure and security exposure and positions are added to those currently under management. This enables certain access points that, digitally, just like their physical equivalent, also require controls, management, and securing.

It is fair to say that the majority of security professionals will have heard of PKI and DNSs. However, very few fully understand them, and even fewer know how to secure them, let alone their criticality and impacts on overall security. They may also not be aware of PKI and DNS misuse, abuse and attacks that have raged for decades (Stuxnet and SolarWinds).

I explained both PKI and DNS to Edward and asked him who within the MOD he thought might be checking these critical areas as both areas, not only the Academy, but also the wider MOD and UK government, were equally exposed and vulnerable to being exploited. I hypothesised that these exposed positions at the Academy may have acted as a calling card for cyber criminals, Russian or otherwise, but could also enable and facilitate digital intrusion. Edward suggested who in the MOD he believed may have caused the compromised area, but nobody had considered our research or evidence and he was unaware if any party was even considering DNS and PKI. Nobody was looking.

I then mentioned my former meeting in Andover with the British Army following a presentation at the Swiss Embassy and how that meeting introduced me to Fujitsu. Fujitsu is a Japanese multinational information and communications technology equipment and services corporation. Fujitsu had won many bids to work with and for the MOD into billions. The Army senior officer said: 'We desperately need your services as PKI and authentication is an area we struggle with Could you meet these chaps at Fujitsu so they can work with you as they contract to the UK Forces.'

We set up a meeting with the senior UK forces team at Fujitsu who, like the Army executives, were impressed with our claims and PKI capability.

They immediately wanted to undertake several proof of concepts (POCs). In exchanges of emails, Fujitsu made it clear they did not want to pay, which seemed rather strange as we, a start up with a world's first full PKI discovery and management technology, and Fujitsu had just signed a UK government contract for the forces worth hundreds of millions of pounds.

After we had undertaken an internal charged POC with a critical national infrastructure company in early 2020, we showed a raft of security issues including Chinese and Russian digital certificates with various privileges. Instead of being embraced, we were almost run out of town, and marginalised by the CNI, GCHQ and the UK government. It was clear that, internally, the UK government had closed ranks instead of addressing the gaping security holes. Holes that no doubt remain to this day.

I explained the above to Edward, without naming names apart from Serco and Fujitsu. Edward was very appreciative of the, as he called it, 'education' and lesson. We have swapped numerous emails and signal messages subsequently. Of particular interest are other reports we have shared with Edward since that meeting and that unequivocally evidence all mentioned parties have DNS security issues rendering them as insecure at their own zones. This includes Fujitsu and Serco, as can be seen below. Both screenshots are dated 25 March 2022.

fujitsu.com

(2022-03-
Description: fujitsu.com zone
Status: INSECURE

serco.com

(2022-03-
Description: serco.com zone
Status: INSECURE

Sat behind these insecure zones of both Fujitsu and Serco is confirmation of DNS insecurity, which is in total contradiction to all basic security advice from government, agencies and even the White House, which on 25 January 2022 published their paper on the subject. Fujitsu and Serco, both major providers with billions in UK government contracts, evidence that neither have adequate controls in this critical area, and all, including the UK government, are 'assuming' security is in place.

The reality is that both are adding incredible security exposure and dangers to every single client. Furthermore, their clients, also seemingly ignorant of basic security, when they suffer a digital intrusion or cyberattack, have no idea where actually to look at, address or remediate. What, if any, third-party supplier due diligence and sign offs are occurring, clearly these are insufficient.

In the case of the MOD Academy, with all the best intentions in the world, I am positive that the MOD tried to address the digital intrusion and, as Edward Stringer said, 'spend to rebuild the Network'. However, in essence, what really happened, as in the vast majority of cases of such acts and remediation, people are looking at, and only addressing the symptoms of the digital intrusion and attack. They do *not* look at or consider the root cause and that root cause is *never* inside the perimeter; it typically sits outside where the servers being maintained and managed by the CDN provider at their DNS positions.

As we have shown above in this chapter, the MOD, Fujitsu and Serco, *all* remained insecure across their DNS at the time of writing. This is more than a year after the cyberattack against the MOD Academy was first discovered. It may have gone on for a much longer period prior to being discovered. Remember that DNS attacks can go unnoticed for years and, if they are simply 'Living off the Land', any cybercriminal, nation state, or otherwise, can effectively be Bcc-ed into all communications.

On top of this, the UK police suffered a cyberattack and the personally identifiable information (PII) data of millions of UK citizens was being offered on the Dark Web until, rather mysteriously, it was removed. I can neither confirm or deny the UK government was requested or forced to pay a ransom for its blunder; however, we launched a threat intelligence program and found a systemic lack of basic security including numerous police.uk websites as 'not secure' due to numerous PKI issues. We wrote to Dame Cressida Dick and the Rt Hon Priti Patel, the Home Secretary, and shared our reports.

The reports clearly evidence a systemic lack of basic security, exposed positions that were easy to compromise and exploit. The office of the Chief Commissioner responded saying they had no problem, and their IT support were dealing with all their needs. Priti Patel's office failed to respond. At the time of writing (1 April 2022—no April fool's joke), the UK Office of Criminal Records, which clearly had been compromised late last year, remains as our report shared, 'not secure'. Its website, www .acro.police.uk, shows that it is indeed the Office of Criminal Records and proudly displays the 'not secure' text in the website address bar. This is national security at its absolute worst and less security would be quite difficult to achieve. The website's digital certificate and configuration errors have subsequently, since sharing information with the Police, been updated and it is now secure.

To provide some context around this, we had been asked to assist the City of London Police in December 2021 (pro bono) as they had some concerns of their own security, even though they had a sizeable and 'professional' team of security experts. Within hours and upon our advice, they closed a major website but, however, failed to realise that stopping the website being accessible did *not* prevent further access as the website, along with others, were simply riddled with PKI and DNS issues.

We provided a free of charge report and were horrified at our findings and shared the report with them. Their head of security contacted us and demanded we retract the report and remove their names contained within it. Instead of opening up to the challenges and insecurity, they chose simply to close ranks and marginalise us, even though they asked for our assistance. In my opinion, this is nothing short of police corruption and deniability.

We then extended our research and when the ransomware attack on Police UK occurred several weeks later, we were not at all surprised. We had extended our research to include the Metropolitan Police and the wider National Police UK. The second and third reports were those that we shared, and which were subsequently ignored. Police UK remain as digitally insecure today as they were prior to suffering a cyberattack as the above www.acro.police.uk website confirms due to being misconfigured. Furthermore, www.police.uk is equally exposed, including having an insecure zone.

What is totally evident and incredibly concerning is that at the UK government, UK forces, the MOD and Police UK, nobody is looking at the critical security area of DNS for themselves, or that of their third-party suppliers. This confirms that the entire country enjoys, at best, an ultra-thin veil of security that, when gently touched—not even scratched just a tiny bit—access to all digital assets across the entire government is possible.

Security levels offered by these organisations is poor, even non-existent. They do not mitigate risk whatsoever, but greatly add to the instability and insecurity of their clients, in this case the MOD, the police, the UK Government and the country. It is nothing short of a national and international scandal that desperately requires addressing. However, as mentioned, government and the agencies, instead of welcoming information and actionable intelligence, simply choose to close ranks and are prepared to remain insecure rather than be exposed for their security negligence.

Whilst the US and UK governments spend and waste billions on *false* security, frequently with so-called 'pet companies', companies that are in 'favour' and that pave that way for future non-executive roles and so on, security, and the citizens of the world are continually exposed and exploited with little to no security or attribution.

Laws need to be made. However, the law-makers often fall into the category above, so it is not the best security that is ever chosen. It is the security that is chosen that has the best personal 'benefits', investors and shareholders: the Old Boys' Club. If this chapter proves one thing, it proves that even when the MOD suffers a cyberattack, nobody cares and nobody takes and responsibility, let alone culpability. Try walking into a bank and causing the loss of tens of millions of pounds and see what happens.

As Ronald Reagan said: 'The scariest 11 words in the English Language are: "I am from the government, and I am here to help. . ."'

CHAPTER 10

Okta Cyberattack

More Basic Security Failures

O N 28 MARCH 2022, Okta publicly admitted it made a mistake to delay disclosure of the Lapsus$ cyberattack in January 2022. Okta said: 'We want to acknowledge that we made a mistake' after only recently reporting that hundreds of organisations, Okta's clients, may have been affected by the cyberattack weeks earlier. The attack was also suggested to have taken place at Sitel, one of Okta's third-party suppliers.

Okta, Inc. is a publicly traded identity and access management company based in San Francisco. Okta provides cloud software that helps companies manage and secure user authentication into applications, and for developers to build identity controls into applications, web services and devices. The cyberattack rocked Okta to the core, along with its investors and clients.

Okta's website states the following: 'The World's #1 Identity Platform. Consistently named a leader by major analyst firms. Trusted by 15,000+ clients to secure digital interactions and accelerate innovation.' These statements now seem rather questionable and hollow, and misrepresent Okta's security capability.

Within hours of hearing about the Okta cyberattack, we launched a thorough threat analysis to determine if Sitel were to blame or if it were a more systemic issue. We did indeed find numerous security oversights at Sitel that included basic security errors of public key infrastructure (PKI) and Domain Name System (DNS). However, it is when we really started

DOI: 10.1201/9781003323273-13

looking at Okta and peeling back what would prove to be an ultra-thin veneer and false security that we started to understand the full scale and enormity of security negligence, negligence that saw a reduction of around 20 per cent of their market capitalisation within days of the cyberattack moving the share price in January 2022 from a high of 174 per share to a low of 142 per share. This was about 20 per cent, or in hard currency terms, reduced market cap by some US$4 billion.

It will be interesting to track share activity from January to date as it would not be the first-time share activity and disposal has coincided with a delay to notify the markets and SEC (Securities and Exchange Commission), whose fines may be a fraction of the monies made on the markets by any actioning of insider information.

We ran our usual checks from domain and subdomain identification to secure socket layer (SSL) tests, configuration and DNS. Some of what we discovered follows and is evidence of an organisation that does *not* deserve customer trust, let alone 15,000+ clients' trust, according to Okta's literature.

The SSL screenshot below is of www.productfeedbacksandbox.okta.com and clearly shows the missing top green horizontal bar under the heading certificate, along with an overall security rating of T which is a fail.

When we looked further, we discovered that the DigiCert SHA2 High Assurance Server CA (certification authority) digital certificate had expired on Thursday 25 March 2021 at 12:00. In other words, it had expired more than a year ago. The date of this SSL security test can be seen as from the time of writing (29 March 2022).

When we look at the actual website, we can see this is a client login website, which is amongst the very worst type of website to be insecure due to the expired digital certificate above. Some clever social engineering and password software and access into the depths of the network as a client, or even employee with privileges can be achieved. Remember this 'not secure' position has been maintained for some 13 months (from the time of writing).

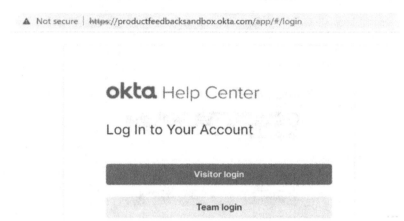

We continued looking at Okta's overall security position and moved onto its DNS position. We covered DNSs in an earlier chapter; suffice to say, a DNS *must* be as secure as all other areas to ensure secure distribution and to prevent Man-in-The-Middle (MiTM) attacks, among other DNS attacks.

The DNS position of Okta.com was found to be shocking as the below figures evidence. The DNS security scan dated 29 March 2022 shows a tale of 13 insecure DNS record positions, three insecure delegation issues, an error and two warnings. It also highlights the fact that the okta.com zone is insecure. Overall, this confirms that Okta's security could barely be any worse and certainly could, and possibly has, facilitated digital access.

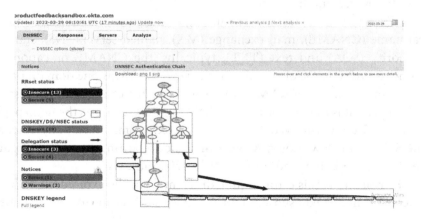

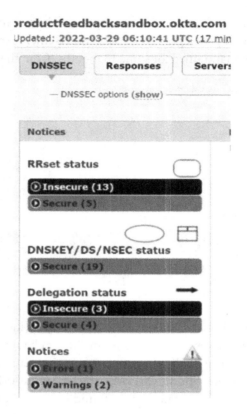

The above SSL showing the missing, critical digital certificate, the 'not secure' website, and insecure DNS show a systemic lack of basic security and controls and all were identified and without too much difficulty by using open-source intelligence (OSINT). We took a further look at DNS and discovered another issue.

A DNS has several records, including web facing (A), AAAA, canonical name (CNAME), mail exchange (MX), named servers (NS), start of authority (SOA) and text (TXT), typically. The CNAME or canonical name record is a type of resource in the DNS that maps one domain name (alias) to another. A CNAME is known to enable changes and access to homepages. It is imperative that the CNAME is as secure as the homepage.

The CNAME of www.okta.com is www.okta.com.cdn.cloudflare.net as the SSL scan below shows. As we can see, once again, the critical digital certificate is missing, and the overall security rating is T.

The reason for this error is quite different from the expired digital certificate from the Okta sub-domain example as this is due to a mismatched digital certificate; although the root cause is different, the symptom and insecure position created are identical.

Internet protocol (IP) 104.18.211.105 and IP 104.18.212.105 are both using a digital certificate assigned not to www.okta.com.cdn.cloudlfare.net but to another domain on Thursday 24 February 2022 at 00:00 Universal Time Coordinated (UTC). It is interesting that this is the date of the first invasion of Ukraine by Russian forces. We cannot prove it, however, because digital certificates that are renewed at 00:00 UTC are usually automated, that is to say they are not manually placed or checked and that would be consistent with why this mismatched certificate which was placed and ignored for the last five weeks, rendering Okta as a company as exposed and vulnerable as its DNS position across many of the DNS records but also its critical CNAME alias canonical name record.

SSL Report: www.okta.com.cdn.cloudflare.net (104.18.211.105)

Assessed on: Tue, 29 Mar 2022 06:57:13 UTC | HIDDEN | Clear cache   Scan Another »

Summary

Overall Rating

T

If trust issues are ignored: A

Certificate
Protocol Support
Key Exchange
Cipher Strength

Visit our documentation page for more information, configuration guides, and books. Known issues are documented here.

This server's certificate is not trusted, see below for details.

This server supports TLS 1.3.

What is abundantly clear is that Okta has been completely exposed and vulnerable and has an exploitable position. It has been exposed for a sustained period of time. It also confirms that Okta does *not* have basic security controls in place, limited to no checks, and no quality control. Yet Okta is audacious enough to declare itself as 'The World's #1 Identity Platform'. The purpose of this chapter is not to beat up on Okta, or to call for a witch hunt; it is to demonstrate and evidence where basic security topples giants and has done so in this case, and many more.

We could cite organisation after organisation and provide example after example of similar errors that have created the initial identification of poorly secured companies and then enabled, even facilitated, digital access and data exfiltration. Such access is typically unknown until the actual attack is identified and the damage has been done. This is because basic security is not being managed, controlled and lacks governance.

'Not secure' websites we term as front doors, insecure DNS we call side, or backdoors. The access to the network, digital infiltration and damage, be it Internet protocol (IP) theft, data exfiltration of personal identifiable information (PII) data or the launch of cyberwars are identical, that is chaos, damage and possible loss of command and control. In some cases even the loss of life.

CHAPTER 11

Stuxnet

I N MAY 2001, JIM GOSLER was retiring from heading up the Central Intelligence Agency (CIA) and the National Security Agency (NSA) as a director of cyber offensive capability. He had been charged with protecting American citizens for decades as the Internet had grown from concept to near full maturity.

Turning to his former colleagues after having started with just two people decades earlier, to what was now a full complement of tens of thousands of operatives, where Jim had seen the split of offensive and defensive go from a 50:50 basis to a now 99:1 on offensive, Jim said with a certain melancholic tone: 'The Intelligence Community needed to adapt, or run the risk of the Internet Eating Them Alive.'

Jim was obviously far more aware of the agency's capabilities and knew much more than he would ever be allowed to discuss or expose. However, not even in Jim's wildest dreams might he have thought that the Intelligence Community (IC) would be able to take things to the full extent that they would over the coming years. To put things into a timeline, Jim's retirement speech was just several months before the atrocities of 9/11 and the Twin Towers attack.

Following the 9/11 attacks, the Bush administration were hell bent to hold those responsible to account and face justice, whatever that implied or meant. Both he and Tony Blair commenced various offensive plans and gained sign off from Senate and the UK government under the auspices of the threat of Weapons of Mass Destruction, including nuclear weapons.

At the same time, America's allies in Israel were also growing ever more agitated, fearing Iran's nuclear programme would see them as a target

DOI: 10.1201/9781003323273-14

and wanted to counteract that by launching pre-emptive strikes and war against their long-time enemies in Iran. Given the already postulated and fragmented positioning, this was seen as complicating an already precarious position and could even would make matters worse. War could always wait and planning of such events are constantly and rather worryingly considered. This was no different and war plans considered by Israel and the US against Iran were pushed back a tad and, besides, the smoking gun was proving incredibly difficult and illusive to find. As history has subsequently confirmed, no Smoking Gun was ever found.

Initially, George W. Bush met with his Israeli counterparts many times and proposed an alternative to kinetic war being launched against Iran in the form of a programme that would go on to be known by its covert, clandestine name, 'Olympic Games', which would become better known as Stuxnet.

The concept at the time, only a few years after the 9/11 Terrorist Attacks, in simple terms was the use of a cyberattack to cause collateral damage against the Iranian Nuclear Program which was predominantly based at Natanz.

The encouragement of using such a non-traditional, and a non-attributable attack was attractive and, besides, as mentioned above, traditional war could always follow as we are now witnessing in Ukraine. If such an attack could destabilise, disrupt or even cause the programme to fail, then the investment in the cyberattack would be seen and considered a worthwhile proposition. Cyber warfare was already in its preliminary stages of discussions even though cyberattacks were confined to the ICs abusing security oversights and errors and using digital intrusion and access to eavesdrop digitally on the world, which included their allies.

Some years prior to 'Olympic Games', the US had researched what collateral damage such technology interference could cause. In March 2007, Mike Assante arrived at the Idaho National Laboratory, where small teams from the Department of Homeland Security (DHS), the Department of Energy (DOE) and the Electric Reliability Corporation (NERC) were in attendance, as were an array of video cameras. At precisely 11:33, the cybersecurity researchers started adjusting the opening and closing of the switches, which in turn affected the speeds to which the diesel machine would typically be used to provide the power for a city. The signals were sent and adjusted rapidly and played havoc on the rotational speeds of the internals of the machine, which incidentally was the size of a small bus. Within a brief period of time, the harmonics of the machine became severely compromised, causing the internals to fail resulting in internal damage, machine breakdown and parts to be shot all over the floor tens of feet away.

This was the first time that code, in this case just 30 lines of code, had been used to cause collateral damage without any external interference and which could clearly take place from miles away, thousands of miles away in fact. Project Aurora had proven that code, when properly inserted, could manipulate and cause collateral damage and certainly became a major cyber offensive capability from that moment on.

In the mid-2000s, with 9/11 still incredibly raw in the hearts and minds, particularly of US citizens, the US were working on several cyber projects. Previously, the US had confiscated nuclear centrifuges from Gaddafi in Libya, and these would play a critical part as the strategy for disrupting the Iranian nuclear programme, which involved the destruction of the nuclear centrifuges, reminiscent of the destruction of the bus-sized diesel machine at Project Aurora. The similarities and timing are all too apparent.

Initially, the US thought, and tried, to coerce (bribe) an Iranian engineer and did manage to recruit a Dutch mole at one point. The idea was to load code onto a USB and plug the USB in to launch the code onto the system. The code would later be called and known as Stuxnet due to two elements within it. The USB and operatives were not as reliable as required and, of course, people's lives were at risk. This was no James Bond or *Mission Impossible* film.

It was decided that between the Israeli and US agencies they would develop code and implant the malicious code into digital certificates, which modus operandi (MO) would go on to be used later in the SolarWinds attack in 2020. Of course, the agencies did not want to use regular digital certificates, immaterial of any 'special' relationship they had with certificate authorities (CAs) they wanted to keep a hands-off position and distance so used two Microsoft digital certificates that were stolen in Taiwan from two companies based in Hsinchu Science Park, namely JMicron and Realtek.

There is a great deal of mystery that surrounds digital certificates, commonly known as X-509 and the security elements of their use, control and storage. The reality is this is heavily hyped as a security feature, however GoDaddy, Lets Encrypt, DigiCert, Entrust and many more CAs have suffered major infiltration and major issuance errors of digital certificates being incorrectly issued in their millions. This did not alter nor change the fact two digital certificates stolen from two companies based in Taiwan was certainly far removed from a more local supplier and, as such, any trail would hopefully go cold.

The code laced within the digital certificate was designed to target one machine and one machine only, namely the Siemens program logic controller (PLC) that was, in essence, a controller that managed the speed of the centrifuges. Consider Project Aurora and the work the changes made to alter the speeds of the diesel machine and the damage to the internals due to the radical harmonic changes whose input was very bespoke by operatives on the switches. The PLC and code programming was to emulate these changes. Stuxnet also utilised several zero days. A zero day or 0 Day is an attack with no previously known examples and with no known remediation.

Public key infrastructure (PKI) is the use of digital certificates and encrypted digital keys which are used to authenticate and encrypt digital traffic, devices and users. PKI became a natural bedfellow for the IC to utilise, but also more latterly, the cybercriminal fraternity as their modus operandi to heavily disguise their malware and attacks as well as being safe in the knowledge very few people have any clue of what certs made up their environment. Nevertheless, the attack required the use of the two stolen digital certificates which were unchecked and, as the entire world suffers PKI challenges due to lack of knowledge and ignorance, the stolen, now laced Microsoft digital certificates were not checked and simply used.

Even though the network and operation were effectively 'air gapped', that is to say not connected to the Internet, this was a favourite easily uncompromised situation. It was, however, compromised by using the digital certificates laced with Stuxnet code.

Once the digital certificates were used, the code used a 13-day delay before unleashing the damaging code to alter the speeds of the centrifuges. The rationale behind the 13-day delay was so that the regular running of the centrifuges could be captured ready to replay once the real attacks commenced. This would lead to major confusion of the operators at Natanz, whilst centrifuges were literally blowing up all around them. The computers would simply say all was running perfectly fine as they were running data from days prior. Now this does sound like a *Mission Impossible* film.

Over a several months, more than 1,000 centrifuges were destroyed and centrifuges that typically had shelf lives of years were reduced to months. In the beginning, Iran's President, Mahmoud Ahmadinejad, believed this was down to internal espionage, and several people were either killed or went missing. It was not until many months later that Stuxnet and 'Olympic Games' was believed, and attributed to, the US and Israel. To this day, neither the US nor Israeli governments have confirmed any involvement in 'Olympic Games' or Stuxnet and continue to utilise plausible deniability. This deniability is possibly the reason most governments and organisations continue to play that card and deny security oversights, errors and negligence. It has become a narrative that leaves the entire world exposed.

It is something of a shame, then, that we have informed several US government offices and the EU Commission that they have woeful security gaps within their own domain name system (DNS) and PKI areas. Only yesterday, a 50-page document was publicly shared on LinkedIn by a known associate of the EU Commission's exposed domains and sub-domains. All have PKI security issues, and all are therefore able to be exploited to enable digital intrusion. Some lateral movement and overall command and control can be achieved as witnessed in December 2020 when SolarWinds (Sunburst) suffered a domain takeover which went on to impact 18,000 organisations, including the US Treasury and many other government departments.

The cyberwar launched against Ukraine, which is now turning into a Cyber Clan war between vigilante groups Anonymous and the Russian group Killnet, is using the very same tactics and cyber weaponry as were designed, developed and deployed by the US and other intelligence agencies over the last several decades, which would certainly have commenced under the stewardship and leadership of Jim Gosler and his team.

In 2008, the same year as Stuxnet was activated, a security researcher named Dan Kaminsky made a name for himself when he discovered a major flaw and security vulnerability in DNS named servers. The DNS is considered the phone book of the Internet. It translates human friendly text (a, b, c) into computer friendly binary (0s and 1s). Computers can only communicate in this way.

Dan discovered that DNS named servers (NS) had a flaw that could be easily exploited across the globe. Dan contacted Dr Paul Vixie and shared his findings. Paul declared the information should not be shared with anyone and that he would get a whole bunch of people together to attend an emergency meeting and summit with Microsoft at their headquarters.

The meeting was hastily arranged and Dan, Paul and a bunch of security, Internet and DNS experts arrived at Microsoft's offices and who all, in a large hall, listened intently. There was a deadly hush and then an announcement that they would urgently address the DNS exposed and exploitable position. Sadly, the fix was a half-hearted attempt which used a patch, instead of a fix. In Dan's words, the exploitable position had not been fixed, just patched up. The exploitable situation would simply take longer instead of being instant.

Dan Kaminsky sadly passed in 2021 and was posthumously awarded and inducted into the Internet Hall of Fame, as Dr Paul Vixie had been several years before for his tireless work in this critical area. DNS, although being designed and one of the Internet's first ever protocols in 1986 was designed and developed by Dr Paul Mockapetris, and along with PKI that was rolled out around ten years later. Both are constantly overlooked, ignored and even dismissed as being not overly important to security and I often find these critical security areas relegated to the 'sometime when' pile.

Dr Paul Mockapetris and Dr Paul Vixie work for companies in the field of security and specifically DNS. The companies cite that over 95 per cent of cyberattacks, malware and bots rely on DNS for successful intrusion and attacks. Both Internet Hall of Fame inductees and members, unequivocally leaders in their field, and decades later, there is still an unbelievable debate of the criticality of DNS and PKI.

Stuxnet, SolarWinds, the world's largest cyberattack which caused 18,000 further attacks, Ukraine cyberwar and thousands of more attacks, all used, exploited, manipulated and abused security failings due to weaknesses and basic security errors of internet assets and in particular, websites, servers and DNS.

Stuxnet hid its code in two stolen digital certificates. SolarWinds suffered a subdomain takeover due to not maintaining basic website security and the use of expired and invalid digital certificates that then allowed domain commandeering and full admin access. Over 70 Ukraine government websites were defaced and lost command and control due to maintaining insecure positions caused by PKI and DNS errors.

Sadly, the cyberwars are continuing as Anonymous continue cyberattacks against Russian entities whilst Killnet, the Russian cyber group, retaliates. Cyberattacks have increased in scale and severity since Stuxnet as the cyberwar attacks on Ukraine prove, however, the MO has changed little since the Stuxnet, highly questionable and quite likely illegal cyberattacks against the Iranian nuclear facility in Natanz.

Until the basic, fundamental basics of security, DNS and PKI are appreciated and understood and moved up the priority list, we will continue to suffer more and more cyberattacks, resulting in a continued dystopian world that sees economies continue to flounder and falter.

CHAPTER 12

Lloyds

Shortfall of Knowledge

'**B**UT ANDY, YOU ARE WRONG', said Matthew Broomhall, the Chief Information Security Officer (CISO) of Lloyd's when we informed him that their homepage was 'not secure'. Matthew took great delight in sending me a screenshot late one evening several days later of their secure socket layer (SSL) A-rated security scan. What I then pointed out to Matthew was that the website was actually misconfigured, negating and nullifying the SSL as null and void. The hypertext transfer protocol (HTTP) did not redirect to the secure hypertext transfer protocol secure (HTTPS) version, rendering the website as relying upon the insecure HTTP version and displaying the 'not secure' text in the uniform resource locator (URL) address bar. This is an amateur's error, certainly not a CISO of a Global player like Lloyd's.

Matthew clearly required an internal education to understand what website configuration was, what security headers were and why they might nullify the SSL security scan he had so proudly waved in a false sense of security and, seemingly, his metaphoric, but hollow victory.

A week or so went by and late one evening and out of the blue, Matthew emailed me again and declared that Lloyd's had moved their website cyber rated index (CRI) from the F and 0, which we had shared with him, to a more acceptable B. When I checked, it was actually a D.

Another few weeks passed, and I emailed Matthew again to confirm the CRI rating was back to an F and that, after undertaking a domain name system (DNS) security test, their DNS CNAME (canonical name)

DOI: 10.1201/9781003323273-15

was 'Insecure', as can be seen below. Websites can almost be considered as living, breathing things. They change and alter; as such, they can become exposed and exploitable. Cyber criminals constantly monitor them, even if the owners do not.

Matthew had to go back to his internal team and Google to try to understand quickly what exactly DNS and a CNAME actually were and what the implications meant. Panic ensued and lots of scurrying around confirmed that our information was indeed correct and that the emails to John Neal (Lloyd's CEO) and Matthew Broomhall informing them of security errors and oversights were correct. Finally, Matthew—although somewhat reluctantly—accepted the errors and finally commenced redress and corrections.

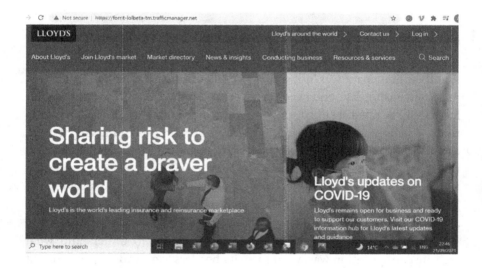

On Friday 30 November 2021, a Thawte digital certificate was placed upon the DNS CNAME. Unfortunately, the digital certificate was mismatched, leaving Lloyd's DNS as exposed as it was when we first informed Matthew and John. Although this is not an uncommon error, it is nevertheless an error that can end up costing tens of millions.

Lloyd's is the world's largest network of brokers, cover holders, underwriters and agents, providing a unique place for collaboration, innovation and knowledge-sharing. I am unsure what security expertise might be shared as it was all too evident that Lloyd's CISO was seemingly and clearly quite reluctantly learning on the job. Seemingly not very well.

I can confirm that, on 29 March 2022, Lloyd's still maintain insecure DNS records, including the DNS CNAME, as can be seen below.

lloyds.com
(2022-03-29) **Description:** lloyds.com zone
Status: INSECURE

For well over six months we had informed, shared evidence and alerted Lloyd's in calls and by email only to be dismissed and marginalised, even after being proven correct and efforts made to correct the security team's errors. To find that Lloyd's are still maintaining an insecure zone is a sad indictment of the lack of knowledge and capability and, sadly, this is not a unique situation, far from it.

By way of an update, as of 10 October 2022, Lloyd's are investigating a cyberattack. We have written to both John Neal and Matthew Broomhall, not to gloat, but to offer assistance—assistance that is clearly and, quite frankly, desperately required.

For the last several decades few, very few IT—thereafter security—professionals actually understand what domain name system (DNS) is, as well as public key infrastructure (PKI), nor the full impact and implications if either are incorrectly maintained and lack secure controls, management and governance.

We have researched well in excess of 1,000 cyberattacked companies in the last few years and each and every one had suboptimal Internet facing website security. This was also the case for DNS positions, with a significant percentage of those companies having various, and numerous insecure DNS positions, including their critical DNS Zone.

We have touched on what role a content delivery network (CDN) provider plays in another chapter. However, for clarification, a CDN simply distributes the data and content of a parent company (client) via their servers, which can be placed around the entire world. The primary job of a CDN is to provide website content to users geographically. This helps in enhancing the server response time, and eventually, the website loading time. CDNs lessen the latency by decreasing the distance between users and servers, which also decreases the website loading time. People are impatient even when a second is seen as a major delay with websites.

All this sounds great of course, and when all goes to plan, it certainly is as you will no doubt have experienced watching movies or accessing websites from possibly thousands of miles away. It is a long way since the bleeping, banging and crashing noises whilst waiting for an Internet connection for Teletext, for example. So, we now have global distribution, and global presence 24 hours a day, 365 days a year with data being captured, shared and distributed globally. There is only one problem: who is holding the CDNs to account for their customers' security, or as in the case of our continual findings, their own insecurity?

This is a major and incredibly pertinent question. A question that makes one think carefully who might really like that data, all of it effectively on a loop, constantly and for the simple price of government contracts or favours for example?

You can draw your own conclusions here. However, we know, without question or reservation, that government agencies have spent billions over the last three decades to achieve exactly this digital control and the ability to harvest the world's data, that is, *all* of the world's data. It is the main reason that China and Russia choose to opt out of the Internet and develop their own to remove the access provided and gained by others. They simply want to have unrestricted access to their own citizens and, in turn, to limit access to others by doing so.

It is all too easy to blame Jim Gosler and General Michael Hayden for their methods and tactics to eavesdrop digitally and to plant backdoors via various methods, including digital certificates. Even with the Omnisec and Crypto AG planting within their Allied governments, however, the reality is that basic security oversights, errors and negligence lies with the owners of the businesses. You cannot blame a tyre manufacturer if the tyre deflates and you do not check the tyre for several years and the tyre fails. It is your job to *maintain* those tyres, just as it is the security team's roles to ensure basic security is controlled and managed. Failure to do so will result in negative consequences. Class Actions may be the last bastion to hold those responsible for Privacy and Security.

There is a laziness in security today, even possibly the wider business. There was even a recent call *not* to fire chief information security officers (CISOs) who suffered cyberattacks under their watch. My first thoughts (and this is just my own opinion) are that CISOs like Matthew Broomhall of Lloyd's should not be in office as they clearly demonstrate they are neither experienced or knowledgeable enough, and let us not forget, Lloyd's is *the* No 1 insurance name in the entire industry and is now investigating a cyberattack. Such attacks exploit exposed and insecure positions. As demonstrated to Lloyd's over the last 18 months, an adversary could have exploited and gained access via a plethora of insecure positions. How can (again, in my opinion) such incompetence be acceptable whilst the organisation remains insecure? It reminds me of the CEO of OFWAT (the water regulator) who said upon receiving our damning report showing all ten of the UK's leading water companies were insecure, 'It is not my problem'! As the Water Regulator, such a statement seems bizarre, or is it just me?

The world is seemingly applauding mediocracy when so much is at stake. This is not a situation where a child is trying to ride a bike for the first time. We are talking major organisations, central banks and governments being hung out to dry due to security oversight and negligence. Much of the cyberwar in Ukraine was avoidable; however, due to basic security errors and oversight, Ukraine government websites were, and still are, being picked off by Putin's cyber offensive teams and supporters like taking candy from a baby. Furthermore, the third-party providers and websites are still accessible to further attacks and infiltration, both directly and indirectly.

The challenge presented by DNS and PKI are not insurmountable. They require expertise, knowledge and continuous effort. Sadly, it appears there are far too few willing to address and remediate these positions. Until they are, they will continue being exposed and exploited resulting in cyber and ransomware attacks as the tsunami gathers pace.

There is a much better way ...

IV

The Ukraine Cyberwar

CHAPTER 13

Why Has Russia
Invaded Ukraine?

Vladimir Putin and Russian military forces shattered peace in Europe for the first time in eighty years when they unleashed a war on Ukraine along with the democracy of 44 million Ukrainians and many more. His justification was that modern, Western-leaning Ukraine was a constant threat and Russia could not feel 'safe, to develop and exist'.

With thousands of deaths in several war-torn, and now flattened towns and cities, along with the displacement of millions of people, both inside Ukraine and beyond, the questions remain: what are Putin's overall objectives and how, and when, might this war end?

The initial aim was seemingly to overrun Ukraine and to depose its government (sounds a familiar strategy and certainly not unique to Russia). In essence, such an invasion and takeover would have ended once and for all Ukraine's desire to join the Western defensive alliance known as the North Atlantic Treaty Organization (NATO).

When the offensive and invasion was launched on 24 February 2022, Putin told the Russian people his goal was to 'demilitarise and de-Nazify Ukraine' and to protect people subjected to what Putin called eight years of bullying and genocide by Ukraine's government. Putin went on to insist that 'It is *not* our plan to occupy the Ukrainian territory. We *do not* intend to impose anything on anyone by force', which seems more than just hypocritical and, indeed, false statements.

DOI: 10.1201/9781003323273-17

You will recall Putin stated that this was not even a war or an invasion. Putin claimed it was merely the action of a 'special military operation'. The Russian propaganda machine and state-controlled media are forced to portray and maintain that same narrative or face dire as of consequences, as we have witnessed.

Claims of Nazis and genocide in Ukraine were completely unfounded, but it was very clear that Russia saw this as a pivotal moment. 'Russia's future and its future place on the world stage were, and are at stake', said foreign intelligence chief Sergei Naryshkin.

Russia's Foreign Minister Sergei Lavrov spoke of freeing Ukraine from oppression, while Ukraine's democratically elected President Volodymyr Zelensky has called for Putin to be held responsible for genocide and war crimes. Zelensky also stated that 'Russia had designated him as target number one for assassination, his family are target number two'.

Russia originally invaded from the north, through Belarus, as well as from the south and east. The fierce and quite frankly heroic Ukrainian resistance has caused heavy losses and the loss of lives for thousands on both sides. It would appear that the Kremlin may have dropped its original plan to oust the government.

Russia's original declarations may have altered somewhat. It declared its main goal was the 'liberation of Donbas', which broadly referenced Ukraine's eastern regions of Luhansk and Donetsk. Back in 2014, around a third of this area had been seized by Russian-backed separatists.

The Kremlin claimed it had accomplished its initial aims of the invasion's first phase. It went on to define this as considerably reducing Ukraine's combat potential. It is worth mentioning that Putin and Russia have also denied any wrongdoing, genocide, rape or war crimes. There is unequivocally a large dose of delusion.

Russia's failure to capture Kyiv, at the time of writing, compounded by heavy losses and subsequent withdrawal from the areas around the capital, has resulted in Russia scaling back its attacks, and with that, seemingly its ambitions. As of writing, Putin's forces were focused on seizing the two big eastern regions to create a land mass and corridor along the south coast, east from Crimea to the Russian border. The mission and tactics seem to be fluid and flexible continually evolving nine months after the initial attack.

Prior to the invasion of Ukraine, it was clear that President Putin wanted control of all of the east, recognising all of Luhansk and Donetsk as belonging to two Russian puppet statelets. The head of the Luhansk had previously suggested holding a referendum on joining Russia, not dissimilar to the internationally discredited vote held back in Crimea in 2014.

At the time, it was not yet clear if Putin and Russia's leaders hoped to control the entire southern region of Kherson and capture more territory along Ukraine's Black Sea coast. Beyond Putin's military goals, Putin's broader demand is to ensure Ukraine's future neutrality. Interestingly, the Ukrainians had offered that in return for security guarantees from their allies, as part of a wide-ranging peace plan presented in democratic talks in Turkey.

Ukraine achieved independence back in 1991, as the Soviet Union collapsed. Ukraine has gradually veered, and leaned towards the West, both the European Union (EU) and NATO. Russia's leader has constantly sought to reverse that independence after seeing the fall of the Soviet Union as the 'disintegration of historical Russia'. Putin has claimed Russians and Ukrainians are one people, denying Ukraine and its long history. Putin said that 'Ukraine never had stable traditions of genuine statehood'. Is it not interesting therefore that Russia invaded, and killed thousands of their 'own', or so claims by Putin would suggest. If Putin's comments were to be believed, it would sound more like a civil war than a special operation surely.

It was Putin's pressure on Ukraine's previous, pro-Russian leader, Viktor Yanukovych, that he did not sign a deal with the European Union in 2013 which led to protests that ultimately ousted the Ukrainian president in February 2014. Russia then seized Ukraine's southern region of Crimea and triggered a separatist rebellion in the east, a war that has already claimed 14,000 lives.

As Putin prepared to invade in February this year, he metaphorically tore up an unfulfilled 2015 Minsk peace deal and accused NATO of threatening 'Russia's historic future as a nation', claiming without foundation that NATO countries wanted to bring war to Crimea.

Russia has been unimpressed with Ukraine's plan for the future status of Crimea, which was seized by Russia in 2014. The Kremlin said Crimea is now Russian territory and the Russian constitution bars discussing its status with anyone else. 'I repeat again and again: Russia's position on Crimea and Donbas remains unchanged', said lead negotiator Vladimir Medinsky.

At the time, earlier this year, part of Kyiv's immediate peace proposals is that all Russian troops would leave Ukrainian territory and the future of the eastern areas held by Russian-backed separatists would be discussed by the two presidents as part of a proposed ceasefire summit.

Ukraine has stated that it will never agree to ceding sovereign territory. However, President Putin would not wish to forgo or abandon any territorial gains made during the war, especially as his declared aim is 'liberating' Ukraine's east. Ukraine has never taken Russia's demand for demilitarisation seriously, and Moscow's insistence on 'de-Nazification' is seen and believed to be merely Russian propaganda. In the words of Ukraine's foreign minister Dmytro Kuleba: 'It's crazy, sometimes not even Russia can explain what they are referring to.'

Putin considers that the West's 30-member defensive military alliance that make up NATO, has one major aim and that is to split society in Russia and ultimately destroy it. Ahead of the war, he demanded that NATO turn the clock back to 1997, reversing its eastward expansion, removing its forces and military infrastructure from member states that joined the alliance in 1997 and not deploying 'strike weapons near Russia's borders'. That means Central Europe, Eastern Europe and the Baltics. Putin sees NATO's advances as confrontational and, even though NATO is seen to be globally supported and objective, it is also widely acknowledged that Washington unequivocally pulls various, and the majority of strings, which direct the focus of NATO's stance and actions.

The German Chancellor Olaf Scholz concluded: 'Putin wants to build a Russian empire. He wants to fundamentally redefine the status quo within Europe in line with his own vision. Putin clearly has had no qualms about using military force in an attempt to achieve his objectives.'

Tatiana Stanovaya of analysis firm RPolitik and the Carnegie Moscow Center suggested that there could be a new 'Cold War' confrontation spiralling in: 'I have very firm feelings that we should get prepared for a new ultimatum to the West which will be more militarised and aggressive than we could have imagined.'

Western leaders are now under no illusion about Mr Putin's willingness to lay European cities to waste in order to achieve his aims. President Joe Biden has labelled Putin a war criminal and leaders of both Germany and France see this war as a turning point in the history of Europe. Before the war, Russia demanded all US nuclear arms be barred from beyond their national territories. The US had agreed to start talks on limiting short- and medium-range missiles, as well as on a new treaty on intercontinental missiles. This agreement has now been shelved and dismissed.

I understand the word and term genocide. However, it is defined as the following: genocide is the intentional destruction of people, usually defined as an ethnic, national, racial or religious group. Raphael Lemkin coined the phrase in 1944 by combining the Greek word genos (race or people) with the Latin suffix, caedo (act of killing).

In 1948, the United Nations Genocide Convention defined genocide as any one of five acts committed with the intent to destroy, in whole or in part, a national, ethnic, racial or religious group. These five acts were: killing members of the group; causing serious bodily or mental harm; imposing living conditions intended to destroy the group; preventing births; and forcibly transferring children out of the group.

The Political Instability Task Force estimate that, between 1943 and 2016, 43 separate genocide events have occurred. This has resulted in around 50 million lives lost. Estimates suggest that a further 50 million people have been displaced by virtue of these atrocities.

The word genocide is used to signify the epitome of human evil and, sadly, few are ever charged with war crimes and genocide. Europe is not new to genocide, as the following list evidences:

1817–1867 Circassian Genocide

1894–1896 Humaidan Massacre

1915–1923 Armenian Genocide

1915–1923 Assyrian Genocide

1915–1918 Greek Genocide

1919–1920 Decossackization

1932–1933 Holodomor

1937–1938 Dersim Massacre

1933–1945 Holocaust

1935–1945 Romani Genocide

1937–1938 Massacre of Polish People

1944–1945 Operation Lentil

1941–1945 Ustasha Genocide

1943–1944 Volhynia Genocide

1995–1995 Srebrenica Massacre.

The first known genocide recorded in Europe began with the Circassian Genocide in 1817 and the ethnic cleansing of the Circassian people by Russians. The Caucasus is a region on the border of Europe and Asia known for political disputes between neighbouring countries. Russia wanted the land to expand her territory and decided to cleanse the people of Caucasus ethnically in 1817 by killing some 400,000 and displacing many more.

The Holocaust is the worst single genocide event in modern history. The state sponsored execution of the Jews in Germany and Europe by the Nazis, who murdered 6 million Jews. The Nazis believed the Jews were evil and had a negative impact on the lives of Germans, which led to the simply atrocious murder of millions. During the same period, Hitler and his Nazi leaders also identified and killed over half a million Roma people.

Winston Churchill once famously said during the Second World War of Adolf Hitler, 'you cannot reason with a tiger when your head is in its mouth' and reflected the statesman's incredulity that Britain would ever consider negotiating with Adolf Hitler. It is completely understandable why the Polish Prime Minster has taken exception to the French President's recent actions and conversations with Putin.

To date, the French President has spoken a reported 16 times with Putin in as many weeks. His declaration and aim is to maintain a communication channel with Russia. War is often seen and considered as politics that simply spill out onto the streets.

As I have said on numerous occasions, propaganda is something to be very wary of. Recently, I saw a photograph used by CNN of a supposed bombing scene in Ukraine with people in the foreground and an explosion in the background. Someone had taken the time and made the effort to highlight a fire fighter in the foreground wearing a US local fire fighter's jacket complete with the local town's name emblazoned across the shoulders. The photo was taken years ago in the US and used in the story. This may have simply been an error; however, it demonstrates how one must be wary of believing everything one sees and what one reads.

What we categorically know is a number of facts, which are irrefutable. The devastation and loss of life because of the Russian invasion on Ukraine is one fact we know. We are also fully aware of the initial cyberwar and cyberattacks against Ukrainian government websites to soften, cause chaos and generally disrupt the Ukraine government and critical infrastructure. We are aware that cyber gangs are piling into the cyber fight, causing further disruption and chaos on both sides, and creating even more instability and uncertainty. This is not restricted to a region but is impacting the entire world.

In another chapter, we consider the warnings of cyberattacks and cyberwar over the last 15 years or so and the brilliant work originally undertaken by the likes of Dan Kaminsky, Paul Vixie and others within the domain name system (DNS) technology world, which is globally acknowledged as a major foundation of all Internet security.

DNS was and is used illegally to gain access to and capture data traffic. It has also more recently been used for nefarious access as DNS attacks are testimony to. We strongly suspect, however, we cannot prove if DNS attacks were used by Russia to attack Ukraine government websites. However, as Paul Vixie stated back in 2018: 'most malware and most botnets rely upon DNS to reach their command-and-control operators, and some use the DNS as a steganographic exfiltration channel for the victim's personal information.' The chances that DNS attacks were used and continue to be prevalent is highly likely, if not a certainty. The DNS positions were certainly exposed, many still are. Dr Paul Mockapetris, the founder of a DNS company, Nominum, Inc., states that over 95 per cent of cyberattacks rely upon DNS. All three of the above are Internet Hall of Fame experts, so who are we to argue with their expertise and knowledge.

I can confirm that, on 5 April 2022, more than 10 weeks since I first informed Ukraine's government along with email correspondence with a third-party supplier managing Ukraine government DNS mail exchange (MX) that this remains as insecure today as it was then. As of editing this chapter on 17 October 2022, I can confirm that they remain insecure. In other words, although a new secure layer socket (SSL) digital certificate was placed on this particular Ukraine government website following our information on 16 March 2022, the misconfigured DNS undermines, negates and nullifies any, and all other, security measures.

A pertinent question to ask then is this. If a company or government uses external DNS resolution services and that service provider misconfigures the DNS, leaving it exposed and exploitable, including the MX, is that provider responsible and liable for digital intrusion and any cyberattacks, including cyberwar?

We will reveal all as the question is really a rhetorical one, as even the smallest of small print cannot negate basic and fundamental security in lieu of providing DNS and content delivery network (CDN) services.

Products and services will constantly change hands, as it is in their distribution that great wealth will be created. That distribution *must* be secure by design, not *insecure* by default.

CHAPTER 14

Sanctions on Russia Following the War in Ukraine

A S THE BATTLE RAGES ON in Ukraine and tens of thousands of people's lives are lost and many thousands more are placed at ever increasing risk, countries around the world have taken evasive action in the form of enforcing sanctions upon Russia in an attempt to cease the flow of capital to the Russian war chest. However, this is hurting not only Russia, but many other countries in Europe who depend upon resources, in particular oil and gas from Russia. Germany derives literally their total gas supply from Russia and with winter looming, it is not beyond the realms of possibility that there may be casualties from hypothermia and the like.

The former UK foreign secretary, Liz Truss (who later became Prime Minister), said that the sanctions on Russia are a 'hard lever' that should only be removed following a full ceasefire and withdrawal from Ukraine. She went on to say the West had to remain tough to get peace. After being appointed as the Prime Minister, she decided within days of being in office to play roulette with the entre British economy placing all on Black, but falling on Red.

Although the Russian invasion is considered to have made significantly less progress than Russians may have expected, the damage is also significant with the loss of tens of thousands of lives on both sides.

So far, over 1,000 sanctions have been imposed upon Russian individuals and businesses, which includes the removal of Russia from participating

DOI: 10.1201/9781003323273-18

within the Society for Worldwide Interbank Financial Telecommunication (SWIFT), the global transactional and payment system.

We looked at SWIFT's own security position and was rather concerned knowing that Russia may see such a move as not only freezing assets in flight, but also preventing moving monies from current, offshore positions to onshore positions and preventing the funding of Russia's war chest. We informed SWIFT who after some period of time decided that the plethora of Internet Insecure positions did not pose a security risk.

Dmitry Medvedev, the deputy chair of Russia's security council, said it would be foolish to believe the penalties will cause discontent in Vladmir Putin's government and claimed this will only serve to unite Russian society.

Interesting, and rather hypocritically, the UK is one of the key countries to impose sanctions on Russian oligarchs, including Chelsea Football club owner Roman Abramovich, Russian foreign minister Sergei Lavrov's alleged step-daughter Polina Kovaleva and billionaire oil tycoon Eugene Shvidler. The UK was originally very keen to allow Russian oligarchs to spend their often ill-gotten millions in the UK to drive up London house prices and to set up tax efficient vehicles with UK tax advisers due to the injection of monies. However, the UK government now wants to act firmly against them all. It is all rather distasteful and unsavoury, as acting blindly as if criminal funds were cleaned up in what has become known as the world's No 1 centre for money laundering.

Mr Medvedev went on to say that none of the Russian businessmen could influence the Kremlin. Mr Medvedev added that Russia could not rely upon anyone and would need to find its own supplies and manufacturers to develop aircraft, automotive and the IT sector, among others.

Russia and the UK have had a tumultuous past. The former Russian colonel and one time spy for Britain, Sergei Skripal, was exchanged as one of the four prisoners that Moscow swapped for other spies in 2010. Skripal was given refugee status in the UK due to having worked with MI6 and settled in Salisbury, Wiltshire, with his daughter.

After leading a quiet life, Skripal and his daughter Yulia were found poisoned and slumped on a local bench. They were believed to have been poisoned by Russian spies. The story drew strong comparisons to the earlier poisoning, and death of Alexander Litvinenko, who was another former Russian Officer, this time from the Federal Security Services (FSB).

Litvinenko's poisoning and death in 2006 was caused after he consumed a laced cup of tea in a London restaurant, which contained a lethal dose of the highly toxic polonium-210. Before and leading up to his death, Litvinenko had made numerous allegations of corruption by Vladimir Putin, which clearly met with Putin's displeasure.

Litvinenko had met with two Federal Security Service agents, Dmitry Kovtun and Andrei Lugovoy in the Millennium Hotel bar in Mayfair on the day of his fatal poisoning. Traces of polonium-210 were found, a short time thereafter, in a property used in Hamburg, Germany by Mr Kovtun prior to his trip to London. There have been other Russian citizen deaths on British soil that seemed to have been swept under the carpet after initial condemnation. The long and short of it is that oligarchs and wealthy Russians were mostly 'allowed' to do as they wished, as their financial wealth defined them more than the crimes they were clearly guilty of, and so they assumed they were beyond the law.

On Tuesday 15 March 2022, Russia officially quit the Council of Europe, the human rights watchdog based in Strasbourg. This was possibly more a case of did they jump or were they pushed? Their actions closely followed numerous sanctions being enforced on Russia by the US President, Joe Biden. The unprecedented sanctions included the removal and lack of access to the US by Russian senior officials. The European Council had previously suspended Russia's rights of representation on 25 February 2022 following Russia's invasion of Ukraine the day before.

The Russian foreign ministry said: 'The course of events becomes irreversible. Russia does not intend to put up with these subversive actions carried out by the collective West in line with the imposition of a rules-based order to replace international law tramples by the United States and its satellites.' It continued: 'Russia will not participate in the transformation by NATO [North Atlantic Treaty Organization], and the EU [European Union] obediently following them, of the oldest European organisation into another platform for incantations about western superiority and narcissism. Let them enjoy communicating with each other – without Russia.'

Russia had previously had its voting right removed in 2014 following its invasion of Crimea. The Kremlin responded by withholding its membership fees. Russia was reinstated in 2019. Money clearly talks.

Let us look at some of the actual sanctions imposed upon Russia as a direct result of its invasion of Ukraine. Sanctions and penalties can be described as restrictions imposed by one country on another to stop it acting aggressively or breaking international law.

At the time of writing, some of the sanctions imposed upon Russia include the following restraints.

Military goods and mercenaries, a ban on the export of dual-use goods-items with both civilian and military purpose, such as vehicle parts has been imposed by the UK, EU and US. This is already impacting Russian manufacturing. Ukraine believes Russia's armoured vehicle factory is already struggling for parts to repair tanks and a tractor plant has ceased production due to parts shortages. This is also impacting the Wagner Group, which is a private military firm with Russian military ties.

All Russian flights have been banned from the US, UK, EU and Canadian airspace. This includes private jets chartered by Russians.

Luxury goods have been banned from the UK and Europe, including vehicles, high-end fashion and art. The UK has added a 35 per cent tax on some imports from Russia, including vodka.

The US, UK and EU have together sanctioned over 1,000 Russian individuals and businesses, including wealthy business leaders, all of whom have, or are suspected of having, ties with the Kremlin.

Assets belonging to Vladimir Putin and Sergei Lavrov have been frozen in the US, UK, EU and Canada. However, the earlier mentioned tax planning efficiencies by legal experts with questionable moral compasses, have 'offshored' through numerous tax havens and effectively laundered and hidden funds, making them hard to identify.

The highly questionable, and quite simply atrocious practice of 'golden visas' allowing wealthy Russians to gain British residency rights has ceased.

The US is banning Russian oil and gas imports and the UK will phase out both by the end of 2022. It will not be so easy for Germany, however, which relies upon both for a substantial percentage of its energy. The EU as a whole gets 25 per cent of its oil and 40 per cent of its gas from Russia and has planned to switch to alternative fuel by 2030, or sooner if possible.

Western countries have frozen the assets of Russia's central bank of US$630 billion, which has caused the devaluation of the rouble by over 20 per cent and led to a 14 per cent plus inflation increase.

Russian banks have been removed from SWIFT, the global transaction system preventing, or certainly causing delays, in energy sales and revenue receipts. Indeed, these are now only being taken in roubles due to the foreign exchange issues. Russian banks have been excluded from the UK and all Russian banks have had their assets frozen.

Many international companies have ceased trading in Russia including MacDonald's, Coca-Cola and Starbucks. Nestlé has also partially withdrawn a number of its brands. Other companies are unable simply to remove all support due to complex franchise agreements, such as M&S, Burger King and Marriott.

President Vladimir Putin has stated that he will make unfriendly nations and companies pay for their imports in roubles. Russia has banned over 200 products including telecoms, medical, vehicle, agricultural, electrical equipment and timber. Russia is also blocking payments to foreign investors and bonds and banning Russian firms paying overseas shareholders. Russia has also stopped foreign investors from selling shares in Russian companies.

Apart from the grey and black markets, and the above-mentioned offshore set-ups, of which there are thousands, sanctions may certainly inconvenience Russia's income and liquidity. However, will it slow down sufficiently to prevent any further progress of the invasion or lead to the withdrawal of troops? I suspect, sadly, no, it will not. Furthermore, as the dependency upon Russian fuel and food resources from Ukraine, the Europe-wide, even global impact, is starting to affect all corners of the globe.

For far too many years (nearly 10) Russia has been allowed to infiltrate the rest of the world (ROW) digitally, with a major focus on the US. Whilst our own governments and agencies used sleight of hand to manipulate their own citizens, Russia was busy setting up sleeper cells like terrorists waiting to launch their devastating attacks upon their unsuspecting victims.

The Russian cyberwar against Ukraine marked a milestone in warfare and, although currently it has not been overly sophisticated, it could just as easily be masking sophisticated malware and malicious code in preparation to close down critical infrastructure, water, power and life.

CHAPTER 15

Eight Years of Cyberattacks on Ukraine

UKRAINE CYBERWAR, AN EIGHT-YEAR BUILD UP …

Ukraine's current cyberwar started some eight years ago and has been 'patched up' using metaphorical band aid plasters in an attempt to cover gaping wounds ever since. As early as 2008, the world was informed of domain name system (DNS) faults exposed by Dan Kaminsky and then others. Sadly, little was done to address this apart from 'papering over the cracks'. Dan Kaminsky and Dr Paul Vixie then alerted the world's leading technical giants of how over 95 per cent of cyberattacks, malware and botnets were using, and relying upon DNS vulnerabilities to exploit organisations. The majority of people chose not to listen; they are still not listening.

With the excellent work undertaken by the Cyber Peace Institute in Geneva, we have compiled a list of some of the major cyberattacks against Ukraine over the last decade. This list commenced some eight years after Dan and Paul had alerted the world to the challenges. We are unable retrospectively to confirm that DNS or indeed public key infrastructure (PKI) issues were the root point of compromise (RPOC) used for these attacks. However, what we can confirm is that the vast majority of organisations, including the Ukraine government, were, and still are, maintaining suboptimal, insecure and not secure positions of not only their websites, but their DNS positions as well. This includes their servers. In addition, the

DOI: 10.1201/9781003323273-19

confirmation that cyberattacks, malware and botnets use insecure DNS exploitable positions, and it does not take a person with a PhD in mathematics to calculate the total sum of 2 plus 2.

In May 2014, Ukraine presidential elections were disrupted due to the government suffering a cyberattack. At the time, the cyberattacks were described as amongst the most severe to sabotage a national election. The campaign consisted of three attacks. The first was infiltration of the central election networks and the deletion of files, which rendered the vote-tallying system inoperable. CyberBerkut, the Russian Hacktivist Group later leaked emails and files as proof of the attack. The election was suitably disrupted, discrediting the outcome and spreading false information. This might have been the first attempt to 'rig' an election by digital means and cyberattacks. This event may also have acted as something of a dress rehearsal for Russian involvement and digital intrusion into the US presidential elections in 2016, with the same manipulation and desired outcome, that of disruption and control. We simply cannot overlook or be naïve to ignore the ability to lay 'plants' for future use. We call these 'digital sleeper cells'.

In December 2015, Ukraine suffered a major cyberattack against the country's power grid, with three separate energy distribution companies in the Ivano-Frankivsk region. This cyberattack is acknowledged as the first cyberattack against a power grid. During the cyberattack the perpetrators also bombarded the call centres to effect a distributed denial-of-service (DDoS) situation. The attack rendered nearly a quarter of a million people without power for up to six hours and impacted 16 substations. This attack became known as 'BlackEnergy', which identified and attacked supervisory control and data acquisition (SCADA) systems. Subsequently, traces of BlackEnergy were found in the US grids network. The cyberattack was attributed to Russia's Sandworm Team.

In December 2016, Ukraine suffered a further power grid attack which targeted the power station of Kyiv. This left the Ukrainian capital and its surrounding area without power for more than an hour. The malware used in this attack was only the second known case of malicious code that had been purpose-built to disrupt and attack physical systems. The malware was also able to automate mass power outages and included swappable, plug-in components that could allow it to be adapted to different utilities and could be used to target and be launched against multiple targets simultaneously. The attack was linked to the previous cyberattacks the year before and was attributed to the Russian group, Electrum, which was known to have close ties with the Russian Hacktivist Group, Sandworm. Undoubtedly, lessons had been learned by the Russian Hacktivist groups from the previous Stuxnet cyberattack on Iran's Natanz nuclear power facility as well as from other digital offensive programs.

In July 2017, the NotPetya attack caused significant issues for Ukraine across its energy, financial and public sectors. The attack using NotPetya wiper malware occurred on the eve of Ukraine's Constitution Day and targeted public and private sector entities affecting around 80 per cent of Ukraine's systems. The highly disruptive attack disabled computers, wiped their hard drives and spread using the popular tax-filing software M.E.Doc. The malware was not designed to be decrypted. This meant there was no way to retrieve the data once it had been encrypted. This also confirmed that access to plain text data was gained, and that data was not only exfiltrated but encrypted by the perpetrators. In other words, the lessons of plain text data, now the absolute favourite with ransomware criminals, once access is gained, is a simple matter of enjoying unfettered access to plain text data. Prevention of access is paramount yet overlooked and continually ignored and nowhere is this easier than where Internet connections and DNS security is overlooked and ignored.

The NotPetya attack spread globally and infected among many others, including Chernobyl and numerous US healthcare organisations. This attack affected 65 countries and 49,000 systems globally. The attack was supposedly a Russian state sponsored attack. The following year the UK's National Health Service (NHS) suffered a major cyberattack called WannaCry, which was attributed to North Korea. The attack had more than a passing resemblance to NotPetya.

In July 2018, a VPNFilter cyberattack occurred on Ukraine's water chlorine distillation system at the Auly Distillation Station. Auly supplied chlorine to water and wastewater treatment facilities to 23 provinces of Ukraine, as well as Moldova and Belarus. Digital access had been achieved and for over several minutes the company's technological control systems and the systems for detecting signs of emergencies were attacked with VPNFilter malware. If it had not been spotted and foiled, the malware could exfiltrate credentials, monitor equipment, adjust levels and render the network inoperable. The attempted attack was attributed to be a Russian nation state attack and, again, potentially acted as either a dress rehearsal or a copycat attack for the Oldsmar Water cyberattack in Florida, whereby similar 'remote access' was achieved and altered the levels of sodium hydroxide from 100 parts per million to 1,100 parts per million, which would have placed human life at risk if it had not been fortunately noticed.

In the second week of January 2022, Microsoft identified and alerted the Ukraine government of destructive malware (WhisperGate) that was targeting multiple organisations in Ukraine, and particularly Ukrainian government websites. The first identification of the malware appeared on 13 January 2022. The malware was designed to appear to be a ransomware attack. However, it lacked a ransom recovery mechanism and was designed and intended to be purely destructive, rendering targeted devices inoperable. Over the next several days, starting on 14 January, the Orthodox New Year, over 70 Ukrainian websites suffered cyberattacks, which defaced, injected code and inserted propaganda, including Russian political statements. The cyberattack crippled much of the government's public-facing digital infrastructure, the most frequently used government websites including the Ministry for Foreign Affairs, the Cabinet of Ministers and the Ministry for Energy, Agriculture and Ecology. The attack has been attributed to the Belarus Advanced Persistent Threat (APT) Group. Further Ukraine government cyberattacks have been attributed directly to Russia by gaining access to web and email servers. Our research confirmed unadulterated access was possible due to DNS and PKI security errors.

In February 2022, numerous spear phishing email campaigns targeted Ukraine energy companies with malicious code, namely Saintbox and OutSteel. The same threat group targeted Western government entities in Ukraine, as well as Ukraine government websites in March 2021. These attacks were attributed to Cyber Espionage Cluster-UAC-0056, who are known to have, and who are closely aligned with the Russian government.

Also, in February 2022 CERT-UA reported mass distribution of phishing emails that supposedly originated from within Ukrainian government servers and which targeted Ukrainian entities. Ukrainian translation software services led to the infection of the malware GrimPlant and GraphSteel. This attack—like those above—were attributed to CEC-UAC-0056 with Russian ties. Just like the FBI servers that sent 100,000 bogus FBI emails, the servers had been commandeered and used for nefarious purposes.

Later in February 2022, numerous attacks against Ukraine government websites occurred including further attacks on the Ministry of Defence, the Foreign Ministry and two of Ukraine's largest banks. The attacks caused further panic and issues with online banking, ATMs and Apps. These attacks were further compounded by nefarious short message service (SMS) messaging that was fraudulent, creating even more panic.

When we first looked at one of the above listed Ukraine government websites in the second week of January, we identified numerous basic security errors including missing digital certificates, configuration errors and DNS insecure positions, which included the DNS zone.

In late February 2022, numerous Ukrainian organisations also suffered cyberattacks, which infected hundreds of systems and networks. The attack involved a new data-wiping malware dubbed HermeticWiper, which is another destructive malware that deletes or corrupts data on targeted computers and networks. The wiper has been detected in Ukraine, Latvia and Lithuania.

Further to the attacks listed above, one of the attacked, critical Ukraine government websites subsequently received a valid digital certificate on Thursday 10 March 2022. It had lacked a valid digital certificate for many months prior to this date and, in some cases, PKI was poorly managed for many years.

CITIZENS OF UKRAINE NOW DESERVE ANSWERS

Here we are in late 2022 and lessons have clearly *not* been learned or the exploitable issues known for decades would have been addressed correctly. If anything, the increases in server numbers and outsourcing to content delivery networks (CDNs) has exacerbated and compounded the exposure and issues. When we started our research into Ukraine's basic Internet security, we were disappointed, but not overly shocked due to having identified similar issues that we had discovered across more than 1,000 organisations that had suffered cyberattacks.

Initially, we started discovering thousands of compromised servers. This quickly moved to hundreds of thousands of servers, then millions. Currently as I type, we are running at over 8 million compromised and insecure servers globally. By mid-2022, we have a list of over 20 million insecure servers. If each server represented a client and each client has 100 staff, the emails and data being sent and received daily runs into the billions sent and received exposed and *insecure*. This includes the Ukraine government and millions of others.

As mentioned earlier, we attempted directly to assist the company which is managing these servers and, instead of being appreciative, they have forced us to adopt a legal position and go down an attorney route. This delays the correction of the insecure position to millions of servers including Fortune 500 and FTSE 100 companies, as well as the Ukraine government.

Are CDN and DNS providers responsible for preventing digital intrusions and subsequent cyberattacks, or even cyberwar? We have spoken at length with Queen's (now King's) Counsel, cyber and privacy attorneys and there is an unequivocal position that immaterial of what 'access' is permitted or provided, that should be under strict guidelines and assurances. To *not* provide basic security measures as a DNS or CDN provider is not only morally unacceptable but is also unacceptable legally.

Should any company or government be compromised, knowingly or unknowingly, due to it DNS or CDN provider's incompetence and negligence, be it by design or by default? I am sure that you will agree, the answer is a resounding no. Never.

Governments and major providers talk of third-party risk and providing audits of the same. Not one, I repeat, not one can with any certainty provide such assurances due to their lack of DNS auditing and lack of knowledge of PKI. Imagine a car receiving its annual Ministry of Transport test car inspection (MOT) by a qualified motor vehicle technician and that technician does not bother to check the tyres, brakes and lights, and provides a clean bill of health only for the car to have faulty tyres, lights not working and dangerously inefficient brakes. You get the idea.

To put this into some perspective, government suppliers and the governments themselves are providing risk registers, audits and certifications that are in effect completely worthless due to omitting these critical areas. When shareholders are provided with annual reports and audits, nowhere is there any provision or mention of these *real* exposed positions. When a company floats or has an initial public offering (IPO), the investors are being misled and that includes many security firms which simply *do not* understand or consider the criticality of their own DNS and CDN position on security and accessibility. One only has to consider Travelex's boom to bust, £3 billion floatation, and 18 months later sold for US$1 following a cyberattack and financial collapse. Or SolarWinds, whose PKI and DNS oversight and negligence led to the digital infiltration of 18,000 organisations and clients, including the US government.

Make absolutely no mistake, basic security errors are costing lives. That is, in Ukraine and the rest of the world, the slippery slope that the Internet and digital communication has the citizens of the world exposed to and also totally reliant and addicted to, is being inclined and greased like some global digital sadomasochistic machine.

Basic security should, indeed must, be by design. Instead, we seemingly accept, even applaud, insecurity by default. Artificial intelligence (AI) and open-source intelligence (OSINT) were designed to improve and enrich our lives; instead, they are used to identify and manipulate vulnerabilities that have been foolishly and recklessly overlooked, encouraged or otherwise, and then ignored. These areas are rarely understood, let alone addressed.

At this rate and trajectory, by the end of this decade, cybercrime could become the world's equivalent to the No 1 in terms of total gross domestic product (GDP). Currently, the US is followed by China, and both are faltering following two years of COVID-19. Cybercrime is currently the third, at US$6 trillion, and predicted to reach US$10 trillion by 2025.

Given the revolution Dan Kaminsky started back in 2008 and the lack of address and remediation 14 years later and pathetic, almost useless address, sadly this fact may be proven correct unless we make some radical changes, and those changes cannot happen soon enough as the war in Ukraine is being played out right before the world's eyes.

I am frequently asked, 'Andy, what has to change to stop this downward spiral of cybercrime', to which my answer is always the same: 'We need to stop, look, listen, and act'. Currently, few want to stop, few want to look, fewer still want to listen, and very few, very few indeed, take any action.

CHAPTER 16

Russian Allies and Enemies

T HE RUSSIAN INVASION AND SUBSEQUENT GENOCIDE against its neighbours, even direct family relations and family members in Ukraine, seem to have stalled momentarily and if anything, the third quarter of 2022 one saw something of a Russian retreat. However, such a situation can often be considered a calm before the storm.

We have heard of North Korea supporting Russia and even mention of a North Korean–Russian cybercrime partnership. Cyber operations have been seen as increasingly important by both regimes as sources of foreign revenue generation. North Korea is renowned for its ransomware and digital currency attacks to bolster its economy.

Panic ensues in the US where warnings by the Cybersecurity and Infrastructure Security Agency (CISA), the National Security Agency (NSA), the Federal Bureau of Investigation (FBI) and the White House continue to alert of the warning of increased cyberattacks on US critical infrastructure and organisations. There has been a steady and noticeable increase in Russian cyberattacks. The North Korean government has been highlighted by US national security adviser Jake Sullivan, who said on 22 March 2022: 'North Korea's cyber capabilities have been working with many organised cyber criminals and nation states, including Russia.'

It has been known for several years that Kim Jong-Un has used cyberattacks and ransomware to bolster revenues for the communist state and

DOI: 10.1201/9781003323273-20

utilising various digital currency platforms to hide the identity and overall benefactors for their illicit gains.

Moscow's cyber ties with Pyongyang date back to at least 2017, when various commercial agreements were put in place including telecommunications and the provision of an Internet alternative. Prior to that date, North Korea had no option but to use Chinese servers. Then, later in 2020, it was discovered that the elite hacking unit, Lazarus, was working with a Russian state backed hacking group. Malware developed by the North Korean group was readily available and for sale on Russian underground websites for Russian-speaking cybercriminals. Remember the majority of cyberattacks, malware and bots rely upon insecure DNS.

North Korea is, in return, provided access to major Western institutions and financial organisations, providing it with greater cybercriminal activities and options against the West, which in turn offer substantially higher opportunities for larger payments, revenues and returns from its illicit activities. Ultimately, Western organisations are unaware of exactly who is attacking them, or from where. They will call such attacks out as sophisticated in an attempt to hide their own incompetence. Their nonchalant, and incorrect view is that attacks are indeed sophisticated, and they do not care who they blame, so long as their own security errors and oversights are *not* challenged or exposed. Insurance companies have, to date, seemingly been more empathetic to such attacks and pay out of claims, incorrectly and further fuelling security incompetence and negligence. Insurance companies—as an earlier chapter on Lloyd's evidence—have little or no real knowledge or idea on cyberattacks and security. For the want of a nail ...

It is *not* their money and, as a certain European professor recently said to me whilst offering me a doctorate: 'We are all kept busy in the Cyber world, so we do not want a silver bullet as we would not then know what to do.' Keep on the treadmill then, as security becomes more a game of chance than strategic or disciplined. This was quite a revelation. I refused the doctorate.

North Korea working with Russia is nothing particularly new, albeit a situation that one might consider somewhat unpalatable at best. In the 1980s and 1990s, under Kim Jong-Il, North Korean government officials were encouraged to raise funds for the Korean Workers Party by any means possible. As such, they engaged in illegal trade in contraband with the Asian criminal underworld. North Korean agents sold drugs to Chinese Triads, Taiwanese gangs and the Russian mafia, as well as the

Japanese Yakuza. During this period, North Korea gained a global reputation for smuggling and drug trafficking. Russia was a key client of this activity.

Let us now look at China, possibly a more natural bedfellow for Russia. China's overall approach to Russian actions in its neighbouring regions has been currently to minimise its involvement. After Russia invaded Georgia in 2008, Beijing refused to recognise declarations of independence by the de facto states of South Ossetia and Abkhazia, for instance. Today, faced with a growing number of restrictions already imposed on Chinese firms by the US, Beijing may be more willing to provide an economic lifeline to Russia, and with President Putin's cronies in particular. China has tended to be extremely critical of sanctions in general, and in particular those imposed by the US on Russia.

Further to the annexation of Crimea in 2014, Beijing offered and provided political support to Moscow. However, China acted with restraint when it came to economic relief for fear of reprisals on China and Chinese companies. It has been thought and considered that China might assist Russia in the war in Ukraine and, only recently, Russia and China issued a joint statement in which China mentioned its support for Russia; however, the nuance is important. China's support for Russia is focused upon insisting that Moscow's security concerns must be guaranteed by the West and opposing the threat to Russia's security from the North Atlantic Treaty Organization (NATO) and other Western countries. It is currently unclear how far China is prepared to go to in this respect.

Whist Ukraine is or was an important economic partner to China and a major supplier of goods, including agricultural products, Beijing has realised the barriers of its influence. China and Ukraine's political relations have been extremely low key for several years, considering Ukraine as having moved more towards the West.

Ukraine has previously provided China with military goods and technology, when Russia was unwilling, or unable to do so. However, the US influence in Kyiv substantially reduced this trade between the two states. An example of this was the prevention and sale of Motor Sich, the Ukrainian engine manufacturer, to the Chinese company Skyrizon.

Many commentators have suggested that the Russian–Ukraine conflict and the Western unilateral condemnation of Putin's actions would drive Putin to work more closely with Xi Jinping. However, currently China has remained somewhat muted, after originally stating it would not support a Ukraine invasion.

Earlier in 2022, at a meeting in Bangkok, Thailand and China announced their support for Russia–Ukraine talks until peace is achieved. The Thai Foreign Minister Don Pramudwinai and his Chinese counterpart, Wang Yi, issued a joint message to that effect. This followed earlier talks in Tunxi in China on Saturday 2 March 2022.

In the meeting, Wang Yi cited the critical importance of China's President Xi Jinping opinions on 1 April 2022, to European Union leaders on solving the crisis given the current circumstances. Wang Yi and Don Pramudwinai agreed to four separate issues:

1. China and Thailand support Russia and Ukraine peace talks

2. Both countries should join hands to avert further humanitarian crisis and provide assistance.

3. Both countries should join hands to curb negative fallout and aid economic recovery.

4. Both countries should cherish a hard-won peace and promote peace and stability throughout the region.

It is worth noting that both Russia, and indeed China, are both currently facing economic instability, Russia due to the incredible reduction of revenues, sanctions and constraints placed upon it and China, after many months of financial stress due to the troubled property sector, which has caused major concerns in recent weeks and months. It was stated in the *Financial Times* recently: 'No other major country is showing deeper sinkholes of economic trouble.' This factor alone may hold back China from further, all out support and involvement.

The Chinese troubled property developers have sought additional local financial support, however due to the sectors uncertainty, many developers have been forced to borrow internationally as opposed to domestically and at higher rates and with much more exposure. Property in China, like many countries, is critical to domestic stability and growth. Around 25 per cent of China's gross domestic product is directly linked to property and around 40 per cent of all Chinese banks' assets are tied up in property. Should a default occur, it could mean a massive decline, potential economic freefall and exposure for China. Such an occurrence could witness the Asian equivalent of the US financial system collapse in 2008.

China is closely, and carefully watching how the United States responds. It has been suggested that this might be a proxy for how the US might react to how the Chinese are acting over Taiwan. The two are not, nor should be conflated, they have their distinct dynamics. Having said that, it would seem that Washington's commitment to Taiwan's defence is somewhat stronger than that of Ukraine.

Today, there are many major clashes between China and the US: the South China Sea, cyberspace and technology, to name just a few. Beijing has certainly reduced its outward investments across Europe. Add the global suspicions of companies like Huawei for digital plants and digital intrusions, intellectual property (IP) theft and personable identifiable information (PII) data theft and the distrust that has built up over the last several decades makes for an extremely uncomfortable, untenable and untrusting position.

On 1 July 1997, the handover of Hong Kong to China took place, which was domestically known as the transfer of sovereignty over Hong Kong and was the formal passing of authority over the territory of the then colony of Hong Kong from the United Kingdom to the People's Republic of China. The event ended 156 years of British rule in the former colony. Hong Kong was re-established as a special administrative region (SAR) of China, and partially continues to maintain its economic and governing systems distinct from those of mainland China, although Chinese influence increased after the passing of the 2020 Hong Kong national security law. Since the handover, there have been many challenges enforced by China, which imposed its beliefs and rule, which has caused much unrest, even riots.

More recently, Beijing has cracked down on Hong Kong's previous liberal freedom which fuelled mass protests in the city and heavy-handed management by Chinese forces which received worldwide criticism and condemnation. Since Beijing imposed a national security law in 2020 that gave China broad powers enabling the punishment of critics and which could, and certainly has had, fundamental life changing situations for the citizens for Hong Kong.

Over the last few years, we have witnessed more than 620 million people contracting COVID-19 in the last two years and over 6.5 million people have lost their lives to the virus. The compounding of this globally impacting virus and economic disaster has been closely followed by the Russian invasion and war in Ukraine, a war that started just days after the Winter Olympics in China had finished. We are now witnessing the largest humanitarian situation in Europe since the Second World War, with estimated costs running into tens of billions of dollars daily and the massive disruption, destruction and prevention of food, water and urgently required necessities will undoubtedly cause many more to lose their lives, totally unnecessarily.

Europe had been brutally ravaged in the first half of the 20th century in the First and Second World Wars. The world has endured a global pandemic and, to all intents and purposes, was starting to come out the other side. Nearly 80 years have passed since the last major war in Europe. Then, Russia invaded Ukraine.

Cyberattacks are rarely classified as 'acts of war'. However, as Cyberwar is now 100 per cent considered as part of any and every government tactical warfare, that situation can no longer be acceptable. As we witnessed in mid-January 2022, Russia launched their cyber offensives upon Ukraine as part of their overall invasion plans. We do not have a digital Geneva Convention, and much the same as genocide is unacceptable under the Geneva Convention, I suspect a digital equivalent would itself be worthless.

As part of any offensive, a strong and strategic defensive position is required and unquestionably complementarily so. By ignoring cyber defence, as the US, UK and Ukraine have clearly done for decades, leaves exposed, vulnerable and exploitable positions, including critical infrastructure. Five eyes and the rest of us are little more than sitting ducks.

CHAPTER 17

Digital Defences Down

I N THE SECOND WEEK OF JANUARY 2022 and, with the launch of the cyberwar against Ukraine in the form of cyberattacks upon 70 Ukrainian government websites, CIP launched our threat intelligence to uncover not why such attacks were occurring but, due to basic security oversight and negligence, just how easily access was provided.

It did not take too long to uncover a plethora of woefully insecure positions due to public key infrastructure (PKI) and domain name system (DNS) errors. Digital certificates are a key, critical part of ensuring basic security and encryption of data both at rest and in flight. Consequently, when a website displays a 'not secure' text in the web address bar as below, it not only flags the website and organisation as lacking basic security, but also sends a clear and loud signal that nobody is looking or checking and will *not* notice infiltration until after the event. Sometimes not even then.

This website is the National Security and Defence Council of Ukraine www.rnbo.gov.ua and connected to numerous other Ukraine government websites and has Port 80 open, enabling hypertext transfer protocol (HTTP) use and access.

Let me explain further what this means. Around 2013–2014, a group of leading technology companies, very much led by Google, noticed website attacks were becoming more prevalent and wanted to 'upgrade' the old hypertext transfer protocol (HTTP), which was unencrypted text, to hypertext transfer protocol secure HTTPS (HTTPS), which enforced encryption, typically using Port 443. Servers have thousands of virtual ports. Billions of people across the globe use the Internet daily. Any, and every web search made sees computers connecting with servers that host the information and shares that information. These connections are made via ports. Port 80, for example, was typically used for the older, insecure, HTTP and Port 443, the updated secure version, for HTTPS.

It took several years to agree to the global adoption of HTTPS in 2018, which was rolled out accordingly. Although the move would ensure greater security, it would also clearly identify those that had not adapted to the upgrade by displaying 'not secure' in the text bar.

A common error is not redirecting properly from HTTP to HTTPS, or from Port 80 to Port 443.

The move was unequivocally the right thing to do in an attempt to better protect website users and visitors. However, like most things in security, it may have been only half-baked. What was required was unilateral adoption and education as most companies needed not only to upgrade their digital certificates, but they also needed to ensure that redirection from the old Port 80 (HTTP) to Port 443 (HTTPS) was in place, along with numerous other necessary security basics including security headers and then DNSSEC adoption to address common errors.

As mentioned above, PKI was globally accepted in the mid-1990s. It uses digital certificates and encryption keys to identify and authenticate devices and users. Think of PKI as a modern-day equivalent of the ENIGMA machine is the simplest way. PKI became the very foundation of *all* security and relied upon carefully selected and appointed certificate authorities (CAs). Think of these as digital passport issuers. The difference is that CAs issue millions and millions of digital certificates daily.

To provide some context to the above, a standard laptop may have between 200,00 and 300,000 digital certificate instances on it, with around 10 per cent of these being unique. Digital certificates typically now have lives of 12 months' validity. As we all know, anything that is annual comes around very quickly and digital certificate renewals are no exception. It is critical that these are renewed and renewed correctly. Otherwise, they run the risk of service outage, renewed incorrectly, or worse.

I touched upon the use of 'stolen' digital certificates that had been used in the Stuxnet attack on the Iranian Nuclear facility in Natanz and this now should start making more sense to the reader. The stolen Microsoft digital certificates were laced with the Stuxnet code and were stolen in an attempt to disguise who was responsible and therefore, who was culpable and to blame. Using newly issued digital certificates could easily be traced. After the Stuxnet attack, it was not long before the US and Israel's collaboration was identified as being behind the attacks. Interestingly, the majority of the US Intelligence Community was put on high alert as they were totally unaware of who the attackers were when it was actually their own people.

Rolling this forward to the world's most devastating cyberattack to date against SolarWinds and consequently 18,000 clients, including the US government, whereby access was achieved via an insecure ('not secure') subdomains (website) as also happened marking the world's first fully blown cyberwar against Ukraine government websites. SolarWinds digital certificates were also laced with malicious code that would become known as Sunburst (Stuxnet to Sunburst, as in the title of my first book) the modus operandi (MO) of gaining access, using or planting malicious digital certificates among the hundreds of millions, even billions of digital certificates would go totally unnoticed until the actual act was instigated and forensic sometime later would identify the cause. The 'perfect weapon', as named by my colleague David Sanger.

In a conversation with a very senior former MI6 officer, he quipped: 'in the Cold War days we had to plant Bugs and devices anywhere and everywhere, now my colleagues only need a digital device, an IP address or Wi-Fi and they can capture anything they want.' Of course, he is right given the focus and development over the last three decades or so within the digital realm.

I cannot confirm or deny that PKI was misused or abused upon PKI inception, although I seriously have my views that it most certainly was. What I can confirm is that certificate authorities are frequent targets for cybercriminals as, in effect, they can provide not only massive intelligence on all manner of companies, but also provide the tools and effectively the 'keys to the kingdom'.

Equally, I cannot confirm or deny that when domain name systems (DNS) were formulated in 1983 and then became an industry standard in 1986, the point DNS become another *backdoor* for the Intelligence Community to manipulate to the point post 9/11 to capture *all* digital data traffic. What I can nonetheless confirm, is the fact that DNS has been used to gain *backdoor* access for many years, and decades, and has become an incredibly popular access point due to many organisations, including governments, central banks, even the intelligence communitys' alphabet agencies, as they do *not* have controls or management in this area, which enables illegal access.

Make no mistake, DNS and PKI were designed and have flaws, they both had *backdoor* access built in, either by design or by default as well as certificate authorities, technical giants, telecommunication, even satellite companies were all too happy to support their governments in their quest to prevent terrorism, wars and even cybercrime. The challenge with this was, like most secrets, they were leaked and the very methods and techniques used for what was originally used to eavesdrop digitally is now being used for cyber and ransomware crimes.

I mentioned that, pre 9/11, only months earlier, Jim Gosler, the former director of the CIA digital offensive programmes had stated that: 'Either the IC would adapt, or the Internet would eat us alive.' Jim was perfectly correct.

Under Jim's stewardship, he had commenced digital offensive programmes from a few operatives to several tens of thousands of operatives. The ratio also radically changed from a near 50:50 split of defensive operatives, to a 99:1 in favour of offensive ones. Defence got left behind and is still languishing in the weeds. It is the main cause for oversight and ignorance of basic security.

Known as Domain Offensive Operatives, these keyboard warriors working for the US and UK governments were tasked with identifying, as part of their reconnaissance, insecure and 'not secure' domains (websites) and subdomains that could easily be infiltrated and accessed. Once these were identified, plants could be made with digital certificates or similar, to route via certain geographical areas—Redmond is a favourite—to enable data harvesting and scanning.

It was not long after such developments and capabilities were being used for more personal, and knowledge-based information was being commoditised by various parties, including social media which was given the backing, and funding by the CIA, among others. In essence, a police state was created.

When any one of the alphabet agencies recruit technical operatives, they will have a list of prerequisites including certification such as offensive security web assessor (OSWA), which teaches website offensive exploitation.

These are highly prized qualifications and those that are recruited, literally without exception, will have such certifications. It should not take too much imagination to understand why that might be.

Let us consider the cyberwar on Ukraine government websites and critical infrastructure. Unequivocally, Russian intelligence agencies, including the FSB (Russian NSA/CIA equivalent), as well as numerous mercenary hackers, were tasked with reconnaissance of insecure and 'not secure' domains and subdomains to gain access. Such activity may have been taking place one or two months prior to the actual attack. Indeed, it is not unusual to have plants for many years and 'living off the land' to enable data collection, harvesting and manipulation without launching any strikes until desired.

The situation as you can see is quite simply digitally very complex, incredibly large in scale and with planted *backdoors* as well as human errors of oversight, ignorance and poor management simply compounds the challenges faced by every security expert. This is made even more challenging as very few people, even security professionals, understand, control or manage their DNS and PKI and, as such, situations like 'not secure' Ukraine government critical websites are overlooked, enabling and even facilitating easy access and simple infiltration.

History and time will show exactly how and where these attacks occurred and confirm the oversights and errors at PKI and DNS, which are all too apparent given the number of identified insecure and 'not secure' domains and subdomains and DNS errors.

We know that many tens of Ukraine websites were attacked using the very same methods and tactics designed by US and UK Intelligence Community agencies. The very same techniques and tactics are taught by various website offensive training companies, and we can finally confirm that many Ukraine government websites were totally exposed where the government was connected and facing the internet. It must not be overlooked or dismissed that the content delivery network (CDN) and DNS providers have also made grave errors (and exposure) on security.

We reached out to several of the CDN/DNS US technical providers on 18 January 2022 to inform, share and offer to assist with the remediation and security errors and swapped emails with them. As I write today, 24 March 2022, we have been forced to appoint a US attorney firm to hold this company to account. I can confirm, the *insecure* position remains to this day and effects millions of companies. By way of update, the week of 3 July 2022, we have engaged with Vinton Cerf, Dr Paul Mockapetris and Dr Paul Vixie to assist with actioning this global security error that effects millions and millions of Internet users.

Inadvertently, our desire to research the cyberwar against the people and government of Ukraine, a cyberwar that preceded the kinetic war which has so far cost thousands of lives and which may possibly cost hundreds of thousands of lives, even more, we uncovered what may be the world's largest technical error and one that has been going on for years.

Today we run the real risk of the current war escalating to a nuclear and or a chemical war and evolve into World War III. This statement is not sensationalist, or incorrect. Shamefully, the vast majority, if not *all*, the governments, agencies and critical infrastructure are *all* maintaining digital insecurity and 'not secure' positions. The overall impact could have a major negative, planet scale impact.

If the world's leaders are unwilling even to learn from the death of thousands of people, it is obviously really hard for us to comprehend. I noticed only a few days ago that one of the 'not secure' Ukraine government websites, www.mfa.gov.ua that was 'not secure' at the time leading up to and including the cyberwar attacks, received a new digital certificate on 10 March 2022 at 00:00 UTC. It had remained 'not secure' for many months prior to the cyberwar attacks, along with many others.

However, it, along with millions of others remain insecure due to configuration errors and DNS insecure positions.

CHAPTER 18

Ukraine Report

Ukraine Cyberwar Using Insecure Websites to Take Over Control

O N THE EVENING OF THURSDAY 13 JANUARY 2022, cyberattacks were
launched against the Ukraine government via its own websites,
en masse. The cyberattacks were termed and considered as cyber warfare. They were of course suspected, and later proved as coming from
Russia, whilst discussions between the two countries and NATO took
place. Whilst this was all going on, Russian forces continued increasing
and building their forces on the border of the two countries at the same
time as the talks.

NB: The 'not secure' Ukraine government website, one of around 70 that
were attacked.

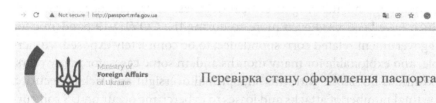

Over the last decade, there have been numerous events in the region, rang-
ing from stand-offs to attacks. Russia has continued to perfect its offensive cyber capabilities during this period. One notable attack included
'BlackEnergy', which closed Ukraine's electric grid when Russia took over

DOI: 10.1201/9781003323273-22

command and control (C2) of the grid's infrastructure. BlackEnergy malicious code was subsequently found in critical infrastructure in the US (BlackEnergy was the name given to the malware first discovered and used by Russia against Ukraine's electric grid).

We launched an immediate research programme into the events leading up to the cyberattacks. We intuitively suspected, indeed knew, how the attacks had gained access and started, as we had already researched over 1,000 cyberattacks. We have been campaigning, informing, alerting and warning governments, central banks and commercial firms over the last several years of their adopted and maintained insecure positions, consisting, in part, of insecure and not secure websites due to a lack of basic and fundamental security controls. This includes the Federal Bureau of Investigation (FBI), the Cybersecurity and Infrastructure Security Agency (CISA), the National Cyber Security Council (NCSC) and Government Communications Headquarters (GCHQ).

Reuters, a credible news organisation, in its headlines, used: 'Ukraine Cyberwar, No Light, No Heat, No Money'. Its reporters are not fear-mongers, and Reuters is not a sensationalist tabloid.

Our research quickly provided evidence of some 100 Ukraine government websites that had suboptimal, insecure and 'not secure' positions being maintained. All were easily exploitable if they have not been compromised already.

For ease, we have tried to simplify this report and its content. Suffice to say, it evidences a systematic lack of basic, fundamental security. Furthermore, it also evidences a shared responsibility and, therefore, potential shared liability. Make no mistake, the government of Ukraine is maintaining and allowing its critical websites, its digital doors if you will, which have been used even more so during the COVID-19 pandemic for all government related correspondence, to be completely exposed, vulnerable, and exploitable for many months and, in some cases, for many years. Ukraine is not alone with this suboptimal oversight and lack of security. The total number of attacks and losses to cybercrime occur on US soil currently running at around 80 per cent.

It is critically important to note that a complete Man-in-The-Middle (MiTM) attack could be simply executed due to these numerous security failings. Through the domain name system mail exchange (DNS MX) insecure record and others. This could allow complete Bcc'ing, unknown to the sender, of all electronic communication, including attachments, both in and out, and amending as desired on the fly (in transit). Imagine a war being played out whereby the aggressor also has full control of the defender by altering the defender's digital communications on-the-fly and thereby influencing the outcome and dictating battlefield actions, all unknowingly to the recipients, and therefore shaping the outcomes.

A grim example would be to give an order to move the tanks 100 miles West, when the battle and access is 100 miles to the East, or to place the tanks at Point X, only to be obliterated due to having manipulated and altering the order and compromising it. Such a capability is similar to playing both sides of a chess game. If you do, you will always be the victor.

The Ukraine's DNS MX record and DNS zone, by being insecure, means it is easily possible to be manipulated to allow the creation of a MiTM attack that could lead to the above outcomes.

As we have previously discussed, a domain name system (DNS) is a hierarchical and decentralised naming system used to identify computers, services and other resources reachable through the Internet or other Internet protocols (IPs). It is often known and considered as the Internet's reverse phonebook and allows IP addresses to be translated from human-friendly names into the numbers the Internet's routers and switches understand.

Let us also confirm what a content delivery network (CDN) is. A CDN is a geographically distributed network of data centres hosting connected proxy servers. A CDN enables high availability and immediacy of web content to end users. The proxy servers around the world remove latency issues for multiple users for high volume usage, as in the cases of government and commercial websites such as Amazon.

A CDN provider is used for this specialised, and invisible to the end user, method of distributing content. The CDN is responsible for availability, which it controls through DNS for its customer. Weakness and security holes in DNS at the CDN mean the potential for a successful cybersecurity attacks against the CDNs' customers. This has been known for many years by agencies, governments and, more recently, cybercriminals, allowing them to manipulate and abuse security oversights that all too frequently occur at the hand-off of DNS from the customer to CDN provider. The CDN customer, if not doing quality control testing, is left unwittingly and unknowingly at risk from the introduction of this hole created by the hiring of, and hand-off to the DNS and CDN.

Below is a screenshot of mfa.gov.ua Ministry of Foreign Affairs Ukraine government DNS records. You will see highlighted the mail exchange (MX) DNS record. The Ukraine government's email is outsourced to Microsoft, and this process has created a DNS security hole that neither side, to date, has identified, addressed or remediated. This one Microsoft DNS record server has been, as our research evidences, using a mismatched digital certificate since Tuesday 31 August 2021. This, in turn, means that the Ukraine government's email could have been compromised with various attacks including an MiTM attacked as far back as 31 August 2021 and is still exploitable.

Among our recommendations, we recommend that the Ukraine government should assume its email, was, and remains, compromised, and that the Russians have read every important email in and out of the outsourced Microsoft email infrastructure since at least 31 August 2021, quite possibly prior to this date.

DNS Records for mfa.gov.ua				
Hostname	Type	TTL	Priority	Content
mfa.gov.ua	SOA	3600		ns.mfa.gov.ua hostmaster@mfa.gov.ua 2022011330 10800 1800 1209600 86400
mfa.gov.ua	NS	3600		ns2.elvisti.kiev.ua
mfa.gov.ua	NS	3600		ns.mfa.gov.ua
mfa.gov.ua	A	300		212.26.137.28
mfa.gov.ua	MX	300	10	mfa-gov-ua.mail.protection.outlook.com
mfa.gov.ua	MX	300	20	mail-esa.mfa.gov.ua
www.mfa.gov.ua	A	300		212.26.137.28

When we then looked at the uniform resource locator (URL) address mfa-gov-ua.mail.protection.outlook.com, we saw that the subdomain resolved as 'not secure', as displayed in the top left hand URL address bar.

This 'not secure' text and warning confirms the domain cannot be trusted, is 'not secure' and hackers might be trying to steal information from the domain, which in this case is the Ukraine government's email accounts, which are outsourced to Microsoft. Access to this domain is potentially far worse than accessing the homepage, as *all* Ukraine governmental email accounts could potentially be compromised and used for nefarious purposes, as well as for revealing confidential government information or sending legitimate looking 'false flag' emails.

As mentioned, such a situation occurred at the FBI in November 2021when they, too, fell afoul by maintaining insecure subdomains, and were hacked. In the FBI's case, its email server was commandeered by criminals who sent under the aegis of the FBI, 100,000 phishing emails complete with malicious links and falsified content. The FBI personnel themselves did not send the emails. Instead, the FBI servers were used to do so because of security negligence.

NB: The 'not secure' DNS MX record.

When we looked at the overall DNS of the same URL, we saw no less than eight insecure DNS records, three delegation issues and three red errors warnings. This DNS could not be any more exposed or more vulnerable.

To confirm, this DNS is Microsoft's for Ukraine government's email. There is zero protection against a successful MiTM attack. None. This position has been maintained since at least 31 August 2021, possibly even before.

This then brings into question liability and responsibility. We know that around 70 government websites were infiltrated and abused, we also know that Microsoft announced they had identified malicious malware on systems. The question one is left with, which is currently unanswered, is what was the root cause? What we can confirm is that all electronic email by the Ukraine government is outsourced to Microsoft, and as such, the compromised DNS has enabled and quite likely allowed an MiTM attack that we believe is ongoing.

We know unequivocally that the attackers could have gained domain admin access and controls, as well as MiTM attacks. We also know they can infiltrate insecure and 'not secure' domains, subdomains and servers. This could be as a direct result of website offensive capability directly into insecure and 'not secure' websites. However, it could equally be because of insecure DNS positions under management, in this case by Microsoft.

If Russia is directly, or though proxy hackers, responsible for these attacks on Ukraine, we strongly suspect that it has simply used regular website offensive tactics as its own domains, subdomains, servers and DNS are equally, and simply quite unbelievably, as insecure and 'not secure' as the www.government.ru homepage displays below. The reality is that every country remains ignorant as to implementing robust, *basic* security and, as such, remains exposed and exploitable.

Cyberattacks, ransomware attacks and even cyberwar will only have one outcome, with the aggressor the victor on each occasion. Until our

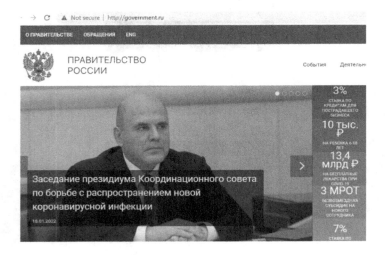

governments, DNS and CDN providers take security seriously, this will continue to be the case. I have always said that weaknesses are in the joints, and security is certainly no different, especially with the plethora of insecure DNS customer to CDN's hand-offs showing a woeful lack of controls and management.

CHAPTER 19

Microsoft

There Is Something Rotten in Redmond

MICROSOFT TAKES A STAND AFTER MAKING GLOBAL ERRORS IMPACTING TENS OF MILLIONS, INCLUDING UKRAINE, US AND UK GOVERNMENTS

On 7 April 2022, the website Bleeping Computer published the following article on Microsoft's identification and effective closure of several websites that had been used by the Russian linked ATP28 Group to launch cyberattacks and bombardment upon Ukraine's infrastructure.

> 'Microsoft has successfully disrupted attacks against Ukrainian targets coordinated by the Russian APT28 hacking group after taking down seven domains used as attack infrastructure.
>
> Strontium (also tracked as Fancy Bear or APT28), linked to Russia's military intelligence service GRU, used these domains to target multiple Ukrainian institutions, including media organizations.
>
> The domains were also used in attacks against US and EU government institutions and think tanks involved in foreign policy.
>
> 'On Wednesday, April 6th, we obtained a court order authorizing us to take control of seven internet domains Strontium was using to conduct these attacks,' said Tom Burt, Corporate Vice President of Customer Security & Trust at Microsoft.
>
> 'We have since re-directed these domains to a sinkhole controlled by Microsoft, enabling us to mitigate Strontium's current use of these domains and enable victim notifications.'

DOI: 10.1201/9781003323273-23

'We believe Strontium was attempting to establish long-term access to the systems of its targets, provide tactical support for the physical invasion and exfiltrate sensitive information.'

Microsoft also notified the Ukrainian government about Strontium's malicious activity and the disruption of efforts to compromise targeted organizations' networks in Ukraine.

Linked to hacks targeting governments worldwide

Before this, Microsoft filed 15 other cases against this Russian-backed threat group in August 2018, leading to the seizure of 91 malicious domains.

'This disruption is part of an ongoing long-term investment, started in 2016, to take legal and technical action to seize infrastructure being used by Strontium. We have established a legal process that enables us to obtain rapid court decisions for this work,' Burt added.

APT28 has been operating since at least 2004 on behalf of Russia's General Staff Main Intelligence Directorate (GRU) 85th Main Special Service Center (GTsSS) military unit 26165.

Its operators are linked to cyber-espionage campaigns targeting governments worldwide, including a 2015 hack of the German federal parliament and attacks against the Democratic National Committee (DNC) and the Democratic Congressional Campaign Committee (DCCC) in 2016.

Members of this Russian military hacking unit have been charged by the US for hacking the DNC and the DCCC in 2018, and for targeting and hacking individual members part of the Clinton Campaign.

Two years later, the Council of the European Union announced sanctions against multiple APT28 members for their involvement in the 2015 hack of the German Federal Parliament (Deutscher Bundestag).'

What the article, and indeed Microsoft, had failed to confirm was 'how' these websites had been attacked, or how many Ukraine government websites were identified as being used to attack the target after gaining access due to being maintained insecurely.

We had emailed Tom Burt, who was quoted in the article and is the Microsoft Corp. VP (Vice President), Customer Security & Trust. My email was dated and sent on 18 January 2022 at 13:54, with the following message:

Dear Tom,

I hope you are well.

We previously assisted MS avoid major exposure of Not Secure 'forgotten' Israel websites that were connected to the mothership (https://microsoft.com)with Pete Bernard and several others.

We have just completed research into the Ukraine attacks and have been asked to author a white paper on the subject.

I have reached out to Ukraine's country manager Jan Peter DE Jong and swapped mails, however wanted to appraise you also that our research shows the Ukraine governments CDN has left them exposed at DNS level which is frequently used by cyber criminals.

Happy to discuss.

Regards

Andy

Tom read the email via LinkedIn. However, Tom did not reply, which is strange as I believed I made the message pretty straightforward and, given the focus and assistance Microsoft wanted to show, along with the support of Ukraine and Ukraine's government and people, seemed rather unusual. I had experienced a degree of normalcy bias and denial previously with the Israeli websites oversight for years.

On 28 February 2022, Microsoft published an article on its corporate website titled, 'Digital Technology and the War in Ukraine'. It was authored by Microsoft's Brad Smith, President & Vice Chair. I had written to Brad Smith on 21 December 2021 with the following email:

To: brad.[REDACTED]@microsoft.com

Subject: URGENT Microsoft Insecure and Not Secure subdomains

Dear Brad

I am writing to you to share intelligence of several Microsoft Subdomains that have been maintained and are Not Secure with all that implies.

Last year's SolarWinds subdomain hijacking evidenced how a SolarWinds insecure subdomain was taken over and subsequently abused. We wrote a paper on the event for the Intelligence Senate Committee which I am aware that you presented at and cited a subdomain hijacking and Domain Admin Access.

We are keen to assist and avoid similar situations occurring at Microsoft.

Regards

Andy

I did not hear back from Mr Brad Smith although, yet again, it was evidently clear we were trying to assist with security oversight that Microsoft and its 8,500-strong security team had overlooked and negligently never checked.

Microsoft started publishing major documents showing solidarity with Ukraine (its client) and denouncing the atrocities of the Russian aggression. One of these documents started with the following:

> All of us who work at Microsoft are following closely the tragic, unlawful and unjustified invasion of Ukraine. This has become both a kinetic and digital war, with horrifying images from across Ukraine as well as less visible cyberattacks on computer networks and internet-based disinformation campaigns. We are fielding a growing number of inquiries about these aspects and our work, and therefore we are putting in one place a short summary about them in this blog. This includes four areas: protecting Ukraine from cyberattacks; protection from state-sponsored disinformation campaigns; support for humanitarian assistance; and the protection of our employees …
>
> As we look to the future, it's apparent that digital technology will play a vital role in war and peace alike. Like so many others, we call for the restoration of peace, respect for Ukraine's sovereignty and the protection of its people. We not only look toward but will work for a future where digital technology is used to protect countries and peoples, helping us all to bring out the best in each other.

We had emailed Brad Smith on 21 December 2021 to inform him of insecure and not secure Microsoft websites. We then swapped emails with Microsoft's country head in Ukraine Jan Peter De Jong, on 18 January 2022 at 12:48 and followed up by sending another email to Tom Burt at 13:54, an hour later.

Brad Smith and Tom Burt did not respond. However, I exchanged emails with Jan Peter De Jong and raised the concerns from our research and findings. On 19 January 2022 at 19:26, Jan Peter De Jong emailed me with the following:

> Hi Andy, we are looking into this matter trying to identify the right people from our company as I am neither competent nor member of our cybersecurity teams. I will get back to you shortly.

I never heard back thereafter from Jan Peter De Jong, even after providing evidence of the security errors made.

What we had discovered in the second week in January 2022, within hours of the cyberwar and cyberattack by Russia on Ukraine, was the fact Microsoft was managing the DNS MX for Ukraine's government across numerous websites. Further investigation revealed that Ukraine and Microsoft were totally unaware of the fact that all emails were being sent to and from Ukraine government websites and servers insecurely due to a misconfiguration by Microsoft that dated back to 31 August 2021 at 00:00 UTC, when the incorrect digital certificate was mismatched on Microsoft's mfa-gov-ua.mail.protection.outlook.com DNS MX version managing all the emails, IP addresses 104.47.18.74 and 104.47.17.138. Due to the mismatched digital certificate, it has a 'T' secure socket layer (SSL) rating and the servers are *not trusted*, exposed and therefore potentially exploitable. Further investigation showed this to be the case since at least August 2019. Such errors enable Man-in-The-Middle (MiTM) attacks and potential domain admin access, as happened at SolarWinds when 18,000 consequential cyberattacks occurred including against the US government and the US Treasury. SolarWinds is also a user of mail.protection.outlook.com, as are VMWare and Microsoft themselves, of course. All of these rely upon the same mismatched digital certificate and all suffered digital intrusion when SolarWinds suffered the world's largest cyberattack in history in 2020. Remember, in the security business we rarely believe in coincidences.

We investigated further and have subsequently, and continually, found more than 20 million Microsoft customer email servers that rely upon this incorrect configuration for security and have done for several years. As mentioned, these customers include SolarWinds, VMWare, Ukraine, the US and UK governments and clearly, millions more. Let us not forget Microsoft itself, which is also using this incorrect configuration for its 80 corporate domains.

It is more than ironic that mail.protection.outlook.com remains insecure because of an error in August 2019, and possibly prior to this date due to the mismatched digital certificate being renewed automatically annually without any checks whatsoever, even after the SolarWinds attack and our informing Microsoft's Brad Smith, Tom Burt and Jan Peter De Jong, and Ukraine's cyberwar being in full flight.

Make absolutely no mistake, this situation is as dire as it could be and affects tens of millions, if not more, organisations, and possibly billions of people globally. The error occurred at least 32 months prior to Spring 2022, rendering millions of Microsoft cloud and mail.protection.outlook.com services as exposed, vulnerable and exploitable. They still are as of the writing of this book and re-editing today (9 July 2022).

The unique fingerprint of the digital certificate is set out below and is the very same fingerprinted digital certificate mismatched and in use for tens of millions of email servers and domains.

*.protection.outlook.com

FingerprintSHA256:   c5dfc706c8aebbb8d55cfc2c89aa993df0c9eafeb-c1b1cf851a3a4babca83cb5

Pin SHA256:

wB+qcVlUxLXcHmk4CF+IClRNjPvp3cgQXiEU84e2rkE=

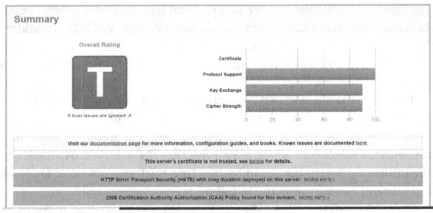

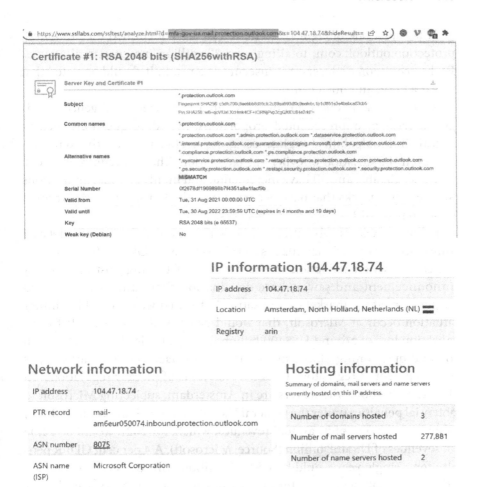

The above DNS screenshot shows IP 104.47.18.74, one of the two IP addresses used for just one of the Ukraine government domains that was attacked, which has 277,881 mail servers hosted on it, all of which are relying upon the incorrect, mismatched digital certificate. The subdomains listed in red above are all also relying on this insecure certificate and are therefore all insecure. The asterisk (*) in front of each is a wildcard. Any domain with an asterisk means that all domains using the subdomain are relying on this mismatched digital certificate and are also therefore insecure.

The second IP address above, 104.47.17.138, yields similar disastrous results, with even more affected insecure email servers.

This is just one of eight IP addresses we have identified for *.inbound. protection.outlook.com, totalling over 20 million insecure mail servers. Each account on each server is insecure as a result. It should be noted that this is a floor, and not a ceiling.

There are many questions over and above the sheer negligence of this global error of unprecedented proportions, including questions such as causal link, culpability, negligence, gross negligence, punitive damages and even the question of cyberwar facilitation. They all require answers. None is palatable and all have incremental and highly serious implications for the cyberattacks that have occurred over the last several years from at least August 2019.

Following Okta's cyberattack in January 2022 and the illegally delayed announcement in March 2022, several weeks later, Okta suffered a market capitalisation reduction in the first day of trading post-cyberattack announcement and saw a share devaluation that cumulatively wiped 21 per cent off the market capitalisation in the first week. Should a similar situation occur at Microsoft, that would be equivalent to a market capitalisation loss of around US$400 billion. It may also lead to a further call for, and questioning of, the monopoly and management of Microsoft, as well as potential regulatory fines for violations of privacy regulations. In the example above, the servers are in Amsterdam, subjecting Microsoft to potential penalties under the General Data Protection Regulations (GDPR) of up to 4 per cent of its annual revenues, which, for 2021, would be a fine on revenues of US$168 billion (Source: Microsoft). A 4 per cent GDPR penalty for a single year would be US$6.72 billion. This does not encompass other Microsoft servers in Europe, or possibly penalties assessed by the UK or the State of California.

In any case, it would be a very uncomfortable position and situation for Microsoft, with major financial and reputational risk let alone future business losses.

We have tried to reach out to Microsoft and would much rather Microsoft listen and engage with us as we might just be the only people in the world that have identified these errors. We cannot overlook the possibility and causal links to cyberattacks. We cannot at this point confirm if the errors were a root cause, or a causal link. What we can confirm is that millions of organisations, including governments, military, Fortune 500 and every Microsoft outlook.com cloud client is currently being exposed, is exploitable, and has been, unknowingly for over 32 months, and counting.

Microsoft states that it has more than 8,500 full-time professionals working within security. Microsoft also has revenues of more than US$10 billion per annum providing security services to customers (Source for both claims: Microsoft). Our informing Microsoft of major exposed Ukraine's vulnerabilities, which remain vulnerable to potential DNS attacks, as well as the vulnerabilities of other governments, intelligence agencies and millions of global companies, many of which have already suffered cyber and ransomware attacks, which is a concerning and dire situation.

In my opinion, this situation not only undermines the fabric of the Internet, but the very fabric of what security stands for and is meant to provide. It is unquestionably a burden to shoulder.

Furthermore, the irony of mail.protection.outlook.com being insecure across millions of organisations and for potentially hundreds of millions of email users cannot be overlooked.

CHAPTER 20

Perimeter Defence Theory in Context

Ukraine

Y OU MAY REMEMBER THAT earlier in the book we discussed my perimeter defence analogy. I would like to use this chapter to give a brief example of how this has worked to the detriment of Ukraine. This will emphasise how serious this sort of security error can be, and has become.

Ukraine has suffered a constant barrage of cyberattacks that have crippled the country's infrastructure and continues to do so. Every Ukraine government website and server that has been accessed, was accessed due to being insecure, or connected to an insecure server which was due to suboptimal public key infrastructure (PKI) and or domain name system (DNS). The digital doors, if you will, have been left not just ajar, but wide open with near complete, total access for anyone willing to cross the threshold. These attacks were not sophisticated, no more than the attack against SolarWinds or any of the hundreds of others were. Sure, the Malware may have been sophisticated; however, the attack and access were not. Ukraine's government websites, network, servers and infrastructure were attacked because they were insecure and easy to attack and exploit. Russian cyber gangs under Putin simply had to identify the insecure access points.

It is one thing for websites and internal networks to be insecure, but it is even more drastic when servers and DNS positions are insecure and invariably insecure for extended periods of time due to lack of controls,

DOI: 10.1201/9781003323273-24

management or even knowledge. That works both ways for a client, or government, as well as the DNS and content delivery network (CDN) provider.

We have recently identified over 5 million (now over 20 million) such insecure email servers known as mail exchange (MX), some of which are used by the Ukrainian government. This means the strong possibility of over 5 million (20 million) exposed and insecure companies sending and receiving billions of emails daily that can be abused, manipulated and altered, resulting in cyberattacks.

To emphasise the possible effects of this, let us imagine a situation where a current war is raging. The Commander-in-Chief sends what they believe is an encrypted message to their general on the front line. The message received says: 'Urgent, move your regiment 100 miles to the *West* to take up position to defend a critical landmark.' The general complies with the order.

When the general arrives 100 miles to the *West* of his current position, there lying in wait is a trap and the entire regiment is wiped out.

Sometime later, the Commander-in-Chief finds out that, due to basic security errors, the order was captured in flight and altered by the enemy. The original order was to move the regiment 100 miles *East*, however, due to a simple Man-in-The-Middle (MiTM) attack, the electronic note had been altered on the fly and ensured the massacre. A single word change from *West* to *East* took seconds and nobody is looking or bothering to check.

When we researched numerous Ukraine government websites, literally all, including the Ministry of Foreign Affairs (MFA) and the Cyber Command Centre, were woefully insecure at both their PKI and DNS positions which enabled, and could even have facilitated, easy access for simple MiTM attacks.

Furthermore, due to the fact we initially discovered the basic security error dated back to 31 August 2021, there was nearly five months of insecurity that could be easily exploited and unknowingly by Ukraine government and the technical providers. Put simply, nobody was looking, nobody had control and management was totally lacking. Complicit? I cannot confirm or deny. Culpable? If by being complacent, then quite possibly. Responsible? Unequivocally.

CHAPTER 21

Cyberattacks against Russia

RUSSIA HAS RECEIVED GLOBAL condemnation for its cyber and subsequent kinetic attacks on the sovereign country of Ukraine. It is also fair to say what can, and has been, used against Ukraine, and thousands of organisations, that is cyberattacks, could be and are being launched against Russia in retaliation for their cyber and kinetic war.

The below http://government.ru website below shows the international sign of insecurity by displaying not only the superseded, outdated, and insecure hypertext transfer protocol (HTTP), but also the 'not secure' text in the address bar. This screenshot was taken on 18 January 2022, within hours of the cyberwar attacks against Ukraine and was still 'not secure' on 27 March 2022, following numerous attacks.

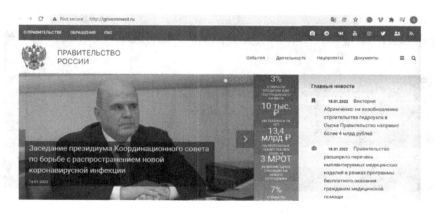

DOI: 10.1201/9781003323273-25

Similarly, the second screenshot below shows http://cbr.ru, which is the Russian Central Bank taken on 27 March 2022 after it too suffered cyberattacks in the previous week. As can be seen, it too is displaying the outdated and insecure HTTP and not the required hypertext transfer protocol secure (HTTPS) to ensure it had a valid digital certificate and that data is encrypted.

I can also confirm that, as of 27 February 2022, and prior to that date, www.cbr.ru was maintaining several domain name system (DNS) record insecure positions. These include web facing (A), mail exchange (MX), name servers (NS), start of authority (SOA) and text (TXT). In other words, not only was the front door visibly wide open by the displaying of the 'not secure' text in the website address bar, but also the backdoors are *wide* open for anyone to launch a DNS attack. It is safe to say these occur where website content is handed-off to a content delivery network (CDN) and is done in the belief that basic security measures are in place and not with basic security errors by default. Remember my saying the weaknesses are in the joints? This is a huge joint that government agencies had questionably used for decades to gain unfettered access and CDNs no doubt have assisted—even facilitated—the proliferation of DNS attacks by their security negligence.

Let me stress something here for the reader: the attached websites are Russia's main *Government* website and Russia's *Central Bank*. Both are key government websites and both are 'not secure'. This makes them exposed, vulnerable and easily exploitable by numerous website offensive attacks including DNS attacks.

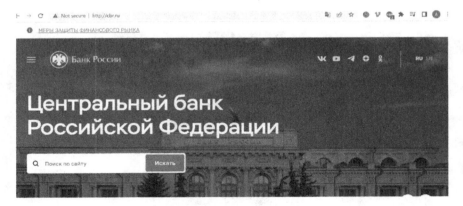

In February 2022, the Hacktivist Group known as Anonymous announced on Twitter that it would launch continued, multiple attacks against Russia and, of course, the way it did this, like the vast majority of cyberattacks was that it gained access via insecure domains, subdomains, backdoor DNSs and servers.

Throughout much of March 2022 and beyond, they have been bombarding Russia with cyberattacks after openly declaring cyberwar on President Putin.

This includes a video on 26 February that was shared, and which went viral across social media declaring and showing: JUST IN: #Russian State TV channels have been hacked by #Anonymous to broadcast the truth about what happens in #Ukraine.

The stunt had all the hallmarks of the Anonymous Group. It was very dramatic, impactful, and shared across all social media platforms. The attack on the Russian State TV lasted 12 minutes, during which time Russia had no control of its own TV station and what was being broadcast. This, as I have mentioned, is known as taking command and control, or simply C2.

The Anonymous Group justified its actions, saying innocent Ukrainians were being massacred and that they would intensify attacks against the Kremlin until peace was restored in Ukraine.

So far, most attacks have caused disruption and some distributed denial of service (DDoS) attacks using basic website offensive techniques and methods. These methods and tactics are made all the easier and simpler to deploy when websites are 'not secure', and their DNS lacks basic security controls and management. A complete C2 of any organisation that has an insecure DNS zone can take as little as two to three days. It is that simple.

What this cyberwar has confirmed and contrary to the false narrative pushed by the National Cyber Security Council (NCSC) and most other agencies, is the use of insecure websites to infiltrate an organisation or government digitally in order to access and alter data and even take over command and control.

In retaliation, the ransomware groups Conti and Cooming Project announced their support for the Russian government. Conti said it was officially announcing full support for the Russian government, stating that 'if anybody decides to organize a cyberattack or any war activities against Russia, we are going to use all our resources to strike back at critical infrastructures of an enemy.' Shortly after this announcement, Conti revised the message to soften it somewhat to state that it would take retaliatory measures in case Western warmongers attempt to attack Russian critical infrastructure.

Conti went on to say: 'We do not ally with any government, and we condemn the ongoing war. However, since the West is known to wage its wars primarily by targeting civilians, we will use our resources in order to strike back if the well-being and safety of peaceful citizens is at stake due to American cyber aggression.'

No matter which way you look at this, it is akin to the Cold War being played out in the cyber realm and the reality is that all sides know that the maintained pathetic level of security and ease of infiltration are doing little other than pulling a few levers and causing some disruption, as opposed to launching the digital equivalent of the nuclear fat man.

On 30 March 2022, Rosaviatsiya had to switch to pen and paper after losing 65TB of data. According to sources, it suffered a major cyberattack on Saturday 26 March 2022. The Federal Air Transport Agency Rosaviatsiya is responsible for overseeing the civil aviation industry in Russia. Its website www.favt.ru went offline two days later and has been unreachable since. 'Due to the temporary lack of access to the Internet and a malfunction in the electronic document management system of the Federal Air Transport Agency, the Federal Air Transport Agency is switching to a paper version', reads the Rosaviatsiya statement signed by the agency's head Alexander Neradko.

The Russian Telegram channel Aviatorshina said that Rosaviatsiya was hit by a severe cyberattack on Saturday 25 March 2022, which led to the collapse of its entire network. Documents, mail and files were all allegedly erased, which was approximately 65TB of data that was lost. According to Aviatorshina's source close to the matter, the agency lost over 18 months' worth of emails and had no back-ups to restore its system. This is simply foolish, if it is true. The source also said that the prosecutor's office and the FSB have been working with Rosaviatsiya since the attack.

Russian media outlet Kommersant quotes two independent sources close to the agency. It confirmed that outages were likely to have been caused by a cyberattack. It is believed the agency has regained its email service and will hopefully restore access to its data storage soon. Rosaviatsiya is posting updates on its social media channels, including Telegram and VK, and linking to its website as if nothing had happened. According to the 'Is It Down Right Now' monitor, it is down for everyone, except for those that know how to access their servers.

The below DNS record screenshot taken on 1 April 2022 is not an April fool's joke. When the DNS zone of any company or government shows as 'insecure', it means that everything connected to the Internet and everything below the particular.com, or in this case,. ru is exposed and exploitable.

In a recent discussion with our top team, where we showed a particular US tech giant as having an insecure DNS zone, as mentioned, they confirmed two, at worst three days for total command and control. To disrupt and cause havoc, only hours would be required.

favt.ru

(2022-(**Description:** favt.ru zone
Status: INSECURE

There are many, many other DNS and PKI issues that www.favt.ru has and I will refrain from listing them here, suffice to say if we can find these vulnerabilities merely a week after the Aviation Authority suffered a cyberattack, although the website may not resolve or seemingly be live, access to the servers most certainly is possible and therefore potentially suffering continued infiltration and damage.

There have been suggestions that Anonymous was behind this attack, although the decentralised hacking group have dismissed a report linking them to the cyberattack. What is clear is that cyberattacks and cyberwar is raining down on both Ukraine and Russia currently and both (although certainly not alone) have lax basic security controls as we continually evidence. Due to that lax and missing basic security, not only does this make them easily identified targets, but easily exploited also.

Recently, Anonymous has confirmed that it is now targeting Western companies who are still trading with Russia, demanding they cease doing so immediately or face cyberattacks. There are many with mitigating issues such as moral, reputational, costs of sanctioning and franchise agreements. The bottom line, I guess, is by now that every government and organisation should start to have become aware that they are easily exploited due to many factors, none more so than the simple fact they have literally been playing with security by having zero controls of the PKI and DNS.

With recent authored reports by the White House Executive Office on 25 January 2022 on zero trust architecture and the extensive paper on DNS abuse by the European Union, one would think, finally, that DNS would start taking centre stage. Sadly, the ignorance and neglect continues unabated, with victim after victim, government after government, and organisation after organisation suffering cyberattacks due to basic security oversight and negligence.

In the two papers mentioned above, DNS is mentioned over 1,000 times. The title of the EU Commission paper, 'DNS Abuse', should be something of a giveaway.

I am personally angry, furious with what Jim Gosler, General Michael Hayden and their peers created and the abuse of digital communications. They may well have been following command, but those commands were highly questionable and today, decades later, are costing the entire world billions daily, and trillions of dollars annually, to cybercrime.

As mentioned throughout this book, at what time in the design and development of DNS and PKI it was decided to *backdoor* and abuse them is unclear. However, backdoored they were and the ongoing Ukraine cyber-war is testimony to the ongoing ignorance and ease of digital manipulation and access.

CHAPTER 22

Global Security Errors

I N YOUR PRIVATE LIFE, you might not want everyone to know everything. Imagine in the heat of the moment starting to get a questionnaire out and asking how many partners, any concerning habits, or if you had any previous sexually transmitted infections (STIs) and so on. You can see how that might not go down well, although, in truth, you know such issues really should be known.

In business, however, you really *must* ask the right questions and ideally before the event if you ever hope to get the right answers or be able to address any shortfalls. In security, it is paramount if you want to avoid having everyone else's insecure position thrown on top of your already, often insecure, and compromised position. I often quote: 'Life is like a game of Jeopardy, all the answers are there, you just need to ask the right question.'

It was earlier this year that a major educational website company was sold by one private equity company to another private equity firm. Within a few weeks, the website company was hacked after having tens of millions of dollars spent to purchase them. The website company had multiple domain name system (DNS) and public key infrastructure (PKI) issues as we researched within hours of the hack being announced. Nobody bothered to ask and check. This was an awfully expensive mistake and, no doubt, a huge loss, let alone the consequential cyberattacks that could be caused due to their insecure positions and all within the US education system. The impact will no doubt be enormous. Recently, Lincoln College had to close following an invasive cyber incident. Unable to afford to replace, remediate or pay expenses, after 157 years in business the college was forced to close.

DOI: 10.1201/9781003323273-26

Let me be candid and make this abundantly clear. Ukraine has not suffered the world's first cyberwar because it had inferior security as compared to the other governments. It has had the same, identical inferior and insecure positions as the rest of the world. It is simply suffering more consolidated attacks, which are exploiting its insecurity. This is not meant as a slander in any way upon Ukraine or its government's ability to secure their digital assets which include their websites and servers, but more a general reflection of global, systemic security negligence. Security and technical debt has been piling up whilst governments, led by the US, happily exploited the ongoing oversight and negligence.

On 5 April 2022, a report was published by *Defense News*, which quoted the US Navy's chief information officer, Aaron Weis, as saying: 'We view cybersecurity as a compliance problem, and it is most definitely not a compliance problem.' Mr Weis went on to confirm the US Navy had approached cybersecurity incorrectly for years and is now chipping away at a new approach that better suits the contemporary environment.

Weis explained that cybersecurity should be treated like the broader concept of military readiness (perimeter defences): 'A more holistic lens would emphasize active cyber management. We have 15 years of track record that proves that the current approach to cybersecurity, driven by a checklist mentality, is wrong, it simply does not work.'

I reached out to Mr Weis after reading this publication and after running some open-source intelligence (OSINT) security checks. The US Navy, along with dozens and dozens of other US forces and government entities are equally as insecure as Ukraine forces and government when it comes to their Internet connectivity, websites and servers. What is more, they clearly *do not know*, that or they are being very accommodating.

On a scale of 1–10, 1 being the best and 10 being the worst, Ukraine government websites and servers score a 10 or a 9 at best. The research on the US Navy's situation has a very similar score. In the last several days I have swapped emails with Dr Paul Vixie – a highly respected and well-known DNS expert. Paul was the person who actually broke the news to Microsoft in 2008 after Dan Kaminsky showed him the DNS faults that could exploit all DNS name servers globally. Paul is an Internet Hall of Fame inductee. I have also swapped many emails with Paul Mockapetris, who was the inventor of DNS in the early 1980s.

Conversations are being held to address the massive gulf between knowing, not knowing, and doing nothing to address the oversights and security issues presented by *not* controlling or managing DNS, nearly 40 years on.

Mockapetris' company, Threatstop, is expert at DNS and has various DNS solutions which of course one would expect. We are hopeful that between us we can assist Ukraine to address some of its security shortfalls. Some uncomfortable discussions may need to take place first and certainly lots of DNS education.

As we had originally researched, within hours of Ukraine cyberwar attacks in January 2022, we initially identified dozens and dozens of 'not secure' and insecure Ukraine government websites. These included the Ministry of Foreign Affairs and the Cyber Security Centre. The basic security errors ranged from public key infrastructure (PKI) invalid digital certificates to DNS misconfigurations and errors. On many Ukraine government websites, the DNS/CDN providers were misconfigured and also were suffering PKI issues. This compounds the challenges. The challenges were further exacerbated as nobody was looking, or aware of them which meant nobody was providing any level of control or management. This is no different from having blindfolds placed over every member of the security and IT team.

Paul Vixie (introduced into the Internet Hall of Fame in 2014) stated in 2018 that *all* malware and botnets exploit DNS vulnerabilities. Add the HackerOne independent security report in 2021, which confirmed that 97 per cent of hackers hack websites and it quickly becomes all too apparent that the known weaponised Internet is being used to gain access. Cybercriminals and cyber soldiers use website and DNS vulnerabilities to gain access and cause damage, create havoc, steal intellectual property, steal personable identifiable information or, as in the case of the Russian invasion, to cause deaths. Deaths are unequivocally being caused by cyberattacks. It may be a cyberattack on a hospital, a water purification company or a critical government entity with knock on, consequential effects.

As mentioned, Ukraine is not being singled out for security failings. The failings are global and impact each and every government, company and person. A short video made by Threatstop, Dr Paul Mockapetris' company, tells how DNS is used for every single connection, for good, and bad and that over 95 per cent of all cyberattacks rely upon DNS.

Dan Kaminsky sounded alarms, that became klaxons in 2008 to Paul Vixie, who then alerted Microsoft, and then the rest of the world of exploitable vulnerabilities in DNS and here we are, over 14 years later, suffering a continuous cyberwar exploiting the very areas that were warned about 14 years ago. A fool learns from his mistakes, an intelligent person from the mistakes made by others, but what are people termed that *never* learn from either? Fools, buffoons, culpable, complicit or even criminals.

Going back to the ongoing cyberwar in Ukraine, and the unprecedented, ongoing cyberattacks globally, our extensive research evidences insecure and not secure positions across *all* companies that have suffered digital infiltration and cyberattacks and Ukraine government websites that suffered attacks. We have evidence of the direct correlation between basic security oversight and errors and cyberattacks. It can often take minutes to find major security gaps and holes that can enable access.

In a major security error that we discovered, and that has a direct relation to some of Ukraine government websites that have subsequently suffered website and server attacks, is, as further research showed, connected with, and to more than 20 million compromised servers globally. The security issue is initially a PKI issue that saw an incorrect, mismatched digital certificate placed on the servers and has caused every subdomain thereafter to be 'not secure' because they have no valid digital certificate due to the incorrect digital certificate being issued.

Furthermore, because like many other digital certificates, they use an automated renewal process, when this server required a replacement digital certificate, it simply renewed the incorrect DigiCert certificate accordingly. The challenge was it was replaced for another year with the incorrect one. This meant millions of servers, and the clients using these servers, are unknowingly insecure for yet another 12 months. We have tracked this as using the mismatched certificate since at least August 2019. It may possibly be for an even longer period. Without address, it will possibly continue auto renewing, incorrectly.

Now imagine a company or government entity has a website (domain) and as the reach of this website grows and different products and services are added to its online presence, numerous subdomains are added. The company or government ends up having 100 subdomains. All require updating, controlling and managing, including the digital certificates. Along the way, the technical department selects an internet service provider (ISP). The ISP provides services for the company or government to access and use the Internet. Contracts are duly signed, and the ISP remains invisible and seamless. The price was acceptable, and they are a well-known ISP. Then we add DNS, who take care of translating the content and data into binary code to enable servers around the world to distribute the content. Then to ease geographical distribution and avoid latency issues, the company utilises the services of a content delivery network (CDN) provider.

All the above ISP, DNS and CDN are household names and provide services to many other companies and governments. What could possibly go wrong? Well, quite a lot actually.

If the ISP provider is not secure itself, that insecure position can expose the company or government. In a similar way, if the DNS is not secure, this can enable DNS attacks including Man-in-The-Middle (MiTM) attacks, distributed denial of service (DDOS) attacks, and many others. Finally, in this chain of website content distribution, if the CDN is not secure that means the servers are not secure and the content being served in geographic areas all around the world is being maintained as not secure, meaning that the servers are exploitable as is the content and data they are distributing for their clients.

You can quickly see how a small issue of a mismatched digital certificate by a company, an ISP, DNS or CDN provider can cause many, significant issues both up and downstream. A pertinent question then is why are companies and governments not taking their, and their supply chains' security seriously? With so many different providers all not taking basic PKI and DNS security anywhere seriously enough, it begs the question, what else other than a cyberattack and catastrophe can they expect?

Since our initial research following Ukraine government cyberattacks in January, we had started uncovering some very concerning, exposed security positions that rendered the Ukraine government as totally exposed. This was not only due to its own PKI errors, but also due to the poor and inadequate security of their DNS and CDN providers. We continued what would quickly become extensive research and started to find many compounded issues like the ones listed above. Plus, many more.

We found ourselves traversing from one Internet protocol (IP) address to another. From one country to another and adding thousands and thousands of servers that were misconfigured leading to more and more. The tally of IP addresses grew and so did the number of misconfigured servers. Before long, the number exceeded 1 million insecure servers, then two million, add another 1.3 million and the total of insecure servers kept climbing. As I write (7 April 2022), we have discovered over 8 million insecure servers which are all exposed to being compromised. This figure has now surpassed 20 million servers, all used by companies and clients including governments.

It does not stop there. For the mathematicians amongst you we should remember that in the case above we cited 100 subdomains. These subdomains are linked and sharing emails and data. Multiply the numbers of users per website, sending and receiving data, and then multiply this by the 8 million servers (now 20 million) and the number of daily digital communication and we have daily use in the billions. And all are potentially easily compromised due to PKI and DNS errors. Nobody is looking. Well, nobody apart from cybercriminals and the Russian cyber military when it comes to Ukraine attacks and possibly us.

Russia has been honing its cybersecurity skills over the last decade or so and has not been shy in practising them widely. It have been taunting Ukraine, the UK and the US during this period and, in the main, getting away with it. It learnt its cybercraft from our very own agencies who, although they may have been the first to design and develop digital manipulation, being first doesn't always count for much when it comes to cyberspace and cyberattacks.

In a separate chapter we listed some of the major cyberattacks in Ukraine that have occurred over the last several months or so at the time of writing. We can confirm that each one had, and many still have, suboptimal security which is either a misconfiguration, a PKI or a DNS issue. We have also touched on outsourcing DNS and CDN to external providers. We discussed accountability and responsibility when outsourcing. It is critically important to understand that one can outsource some elements of authority and accountability, but you cannot outsource overall accountability nor responsibility. There is a very critical distinction and, sadly, the attorneys being called in to address these issues are having to consider responsibility and liability. Again, these are very important distinctions.

Let us take the situation in Ukraine. Let us agree that www.mfa.gov.ua is managing its website and it was were accountable and responsible for the security of the website, which included the configuration and validity, including the SSL/TLS digital certificates.

The DNS and CDN providers were handed the content and their provided servers distributed the content, but now as binary code allowing servers to share the data and communicate with one another and then resolve that content locally for users. There is a major question around responsibility when data is handed-off to a DNS/CDN provider and we certainly have our beliefs, as do our attorneys.

The question we pose is simple: if a company suffers a digital intrusion that can be shown to have been a DNS attack or a government that had a DDoS or MiTM attack that heralded from a DNS attack and access that was gained via the DNS/CDN provider, is that provider then responsible and liable for the digital access, and for any and all subsequent cyber-attacks, IP or Personal Identifiable Information (PII) theft, costs and losses?

This is another really key issue and, depending upon the outcome our attorneys are currently drafting correspondence for a major US tech giant to consider, as there is also a difference between culpability and causal links. In our opinion, it is *never* okay for a provider, ISP, DNS or CDN provider not to control and manage their security adequately and securely. By not doing so, they simply reinforce their clients insecurity by default and frequently unknowingly. Imagine spending a billion dollars, like Bank of America on cybersecurity, only to find out your CDN enabled a huge DNS attack due to their insecure DNS records, NS and CNAME.

Let us consider another example. Take a government website that displays a 'not secure' text in the URL address bar due to a misconfiguration or an invalid digital certificate. Then, sometime later that same government suffers a digital intrusion. This then leads to a major cyberattack, with the accompanying disruption, costs and losses.

During the post-mortem sometime later, it is discovered that an A, MX, or CNAME DNS record was misconfigured by the DNS/CDN provider and the server, due to the misconfiguration, was attacked in a typical MiTM DNS attack, which was then used to gain server access and infiltrate the government, and exfiltrate data.

We have all variants in play right now. We have authorisation, accountability, responsibility and liability to consider. Was the government website targeted because it was flying the 'not secure' flag, which can be considered as a causal link. Was the government attacked because a DNS threat analysis provided evidence of insecure DNS, which could enable a successful MiTM attack?

Clearly, there is a huge difference between causal and culpable and one for the attorneys to work out for sure. What this proves, however, is—as my dear old friend Jeff always used to say to me many years ago—when attorneys must read the small print in a contract, you know something has gone dreadfully wrong. He was certainly right.

In the examples above, the government has suffered a cyberattack and loss. It has incurred costs, reputational damage and lost trust from its citizens, let us not forget, voting citizens. It takes the brunt of the damage no matter what the root cause was or what occurs thereafter. People always remember the first, and this is no different. Sure, the attorneys may sort out something down the line; however, the damage has been done.

Now lay the last several paragraphs over the Ukraine government as it has unequivocally suffered multiple website attacks and intrusions. It certainly maintained many of its websites as insecure and displaying the international flag of 'not secure' due to its own internal errors. It is accountable and responsible. There are also major security errors by Ukraine government third-party DNS/CDN suppliers.

People have lost their lives. In fact, thousands of people have lost their lives and with government websites defaced, altered and then unavailable, communication has been affected as Ukraine's infrastructure has been adversely affected.

Now we have an even more complex situation of causal links and culpability, only this time it potentially goes all the way to collateral damage and the loss of life. We have, over the last several decades, built and totally depended upon the digital world we have created. As Dr Paul Mockapetris stated: 'Everything Good, and Bad on the Internet, the Internet our digital world relies and depends upon DNS.'

It is possibly easier then to suggest that if a company knowingly, or otherwise, exposes its client, paying or otherwise, to DNS attacks due to its basic security failings, that it is culpable, responsible and liable? Is there any other way to see this and. as a result, we would urge every organisation using such services to ensure it knows exactly how secure—or not—its service providers are?

This is not a situation that should ever be assumed or ignored unless digital intrusion is part of an overall strategy and desired outcome.

Conclusion

As I have already said, sometimes separating the 'good guys' from the 'bad guys' is really quite an impossible task, and one does not need to go too far back in history to recall major espionage, double agents and national security being compromised for wads of cash (now bitcoin no doubt). The difference today is that we are talking billions of dollars in the balance, with trillions of dollars being moved on a daily basis and much of our infrastructure is wide open to cyberattacks due to basic security oversight and negligence. Literally all digital activity is done so *insecurely one way or another.*

Education, education, education ... We urgently need companies and governments to stop hypothesising and take a further step to cease the rhetoric and *fait accompli* post-cyberattack measures and frameworks and start putting and ensuring preventative measures are in place. I often use another term: 'I do not need to outrun the hungry lion, just outrun you.'

Security is much the same. A lion does not look to attack the strongest of the herd; it will pick off the weakest and most frail of the herd. As callous as that may appear, that is exactly how things are: The Circle of Life, if you will.

We must remember who started domain name systems (DNS) and public key infrastructure (PKI), and who started abusing DNS and PKI, and why those people might *not* want the rest of the world to ensure these areas are maintained as 'Insecure'?

That individual, the cybercriminal, will *not* select and avoid on purpose Company A over Company B if Company A demonstrates a really strong and secure position when Company B has a raft of basic security errors and is still using hypertext transfer protocol (HTTP) because of a misconfiguration or an expired digital certificate. The cybercriminal will simply go after Company B as the weakest and most insecure. Sadly, there are millions upon millions of Company B's that are either complacent, complicit or lack the capability to ensure their multi-billion-dollar company, bank, energy provider, nuclear facility or government that is incredibly exposed and exploitable due to basic security negligence.

DOI: 10.1201/9781003323273-27

The term 'when' not 'if' a cyberattack occurs against a company was coined many years ago along with the phrase: 'there are two kinds of companies, those that have been hacked, and those that do not yet know they have been hacked.' In the main, I cannot argue with either as, for decades, companies and governments around the world have 'plugged in' to the Internet and been completely ignorant to what that meant and what exposure it created and enabled.

I am at a loss to explain the sheer scale of negligence across all industries, sectors and governments other than the narrative pushed by the agencies. Shockingly, as this book evidences, insecurity is so widespread. The fact DNS has been around for nearly 40 years and PKI for nearly 30 years yet both are insecurely maintained simply beggars belief.

Our governments have unquestionably subscribed to the belief that defence does not win wars, and that the best defence is offence, rather like a Mike Tyson taking on a Muhammed Ali. An out and out fighter versus a boxer. One cannot argue with that too harshly, however. Offence should not be at the total expense of defence. At what stage that should be adjusted to account for all out cyberwar is an uncomfortable question for the majority of leaders both in the current theatre of war, but also as governments and intelligence agencies move forward in the new theatre of cyberwar.

This book, *Digital Blood on Their Hands*, shockingly shows the sheer devastation including the loss of countless lives that can occur as a result of security oversight and negligence. Unequivocally, our threat analysis and discoveries constitute one of the world's possible worst cases of security negligence and lack of management oversight, as well as negligence; management oversight which may have had led to many of the world's largest losses. We cannot rule out causal links to direct cyberattacks because of this security negligence by a third-party global supplier.

We have entered a new era, one that relies upon keyboard warriors and digital soldiers. An era where attribution is rare and the way of life can be altered by the depression of a single key on a keyboard. We have made life easier to communicate, shop and buy online. At the same time, due to arrogance and foolishness, our intelligence communities wear blinkers and side with technical giants, telecommunications companies, software and hardware providers to facilitate digital eavesdropping and digital intrusion. That same abuse, manipulation and access via planted backdoors are now used to attack the digital trust of the world, undermining the very fabric of humanity and, as a result, we have new constants, cyberattacks and cyberwar.

The reliance and errors made by those listed above did not consider, nor allow for continuous human errors and negligence. A simple check after automatic renewal of a digital certificate the first time it was used would have caught this. Blind faith in automation and an inattentive and oblivious management failings have created and made this situation possible.

The keyboard has unequivocally become mightier than the sword.

Afterword

Rogers

O<small>N</small> 8 J<small>ULY</small> 2022, Rogers, Canada's largest Internet Service Provider (ISP) and communications company, suffered a service outage that lasted for 19 hours and impacted over 25 per cent of Canada's population. The outage impacted Rogers' subsidiary companies, Rogers Wireless, Fido, Cityfone and Chatr. Rogers is no strangers to digital service outages, having suffered a similar event in April 2021. The outage affected the Canadian Government.

Rogers also suffered a major cyberattack in March 2016, when it confirmed the event to *Bank Info Security*, the digital magazine. The hack was reportedly blamed upon a social engineering hack claimed by TeamHans, who were vocal about targeting Rogers.

Rogers and the targeted employees refused to pay the ransom in Bitcoin, so the data was leaked online. Rogers played down the attack, citing only 50 to 70 small and medium-sized companies had their data exfiltrated.

As mentioned, Rogers is no stranger to service outages and digital intrusion; however, now we believe that we have uncovered that the latest cyberattack (outage as the world was informed) was for various reasons which might include Rogers' current bid to acquire Shaw's, its closest telecommunications competitor, for approximately US$16 billion, was actually a cyberattack by Russia as opposed to a service outage.

The latest digital incident occurred on Friday 8 July 2022 and had been preceded by a week of Canadian debates and unrest as the Canadian Government, including Prime Minster Justin Trudeau, debated over the legitimacy and sanctions of returning the repaired, critical Russian-owned

DOI: 10.1201/9781003323273-28

Gazprom turbine. The President of Ukraine personally requested that Canada observe and comply with the sanctions against Russia by not returning the turbine as opposed to further fueling the war machine.

In an interview in Moscow only a day following the Rogers incident, *The Beaverton* publication said in its article on an interview with the Russian President that 'Vladimir Putin determined that allowing the existence of Rogers Telecommunications as a major provider in Canada was much better than launching a cyberattack against the country.'

He said, 'Why hack into the country's power grid when this company (Rogers) can do a much better job at paralyzing the Canadian Infrastructure and economy?'

Putin expressed his admiration for the NATO country's ability to concentrate tremendous power in unaccountable corporate oligarchs whose incompetence is far more efficient at disabling critical infrastructure than cruise missile strikes hitting major telecommunication sites.

'Call off the attack, and purchase some more stock in Rogers', Putin added. The federal government promised to hold Rogers to account.

On 10 July 2022, I wrote to Robert Depatie via LinkedIn introducing myself and what we had discovered so far as Internet facing security was concerned. Overnight, Robert accepted my connection request and I sent further information in an email. My email included screenshots of insecure domain name systems (DNS) and evidence of a woefully insecure position across all areas including the critical DNS zone. Of course, my being in Windsor and Robert being in Quebec there was a slight time difference and delay; however, we (CIP) were convinced that Russia had sent a clear message by undertaking a 'proof-of-concept' warning attack against Rogers and clearly signalled 'send our turbine back or there would be further outages to Rogers and others'.

Robert did not respond to my email which seemed strange as my original email left no confusion about the reason for messaging and our research findings.

My first email to Robert dated 11 July 2022 was one business day following their incident.

> Dear Robert
> Further to our connection on LinkedIn and my most concerning inmail sent to you over the weekend evidencing highly exposed and insecure positions across Rogers, the attached are equally of concern if Rogers are going to acquire Shaw.

We are spinning plates at a rate of knots. The Siemens and Canadian Government release of Russia's repaired turbine I believe might be directly related to the digital intrusion at Rogers. One can expect further reprisals and attacks. The situation and insecurity we have highlighted will unequivocally provide unbridled access for cybercriminals.

We are not under any agreement or NDA's. You have my word that we will not do anything for a period of a week which provides enough time for Rogers to engage with us or choose to ignore us.

Yours sincerely.

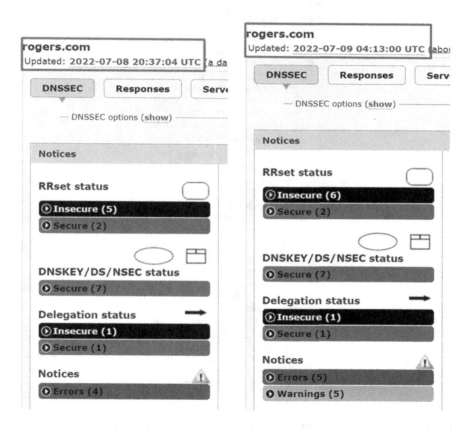

The above DNS screenshots show on the left-hand side, dated 8 July 2022, the day of the 'service outage' that the suboptimal position is clearly bad. However, now look at the screenshot on the right-hand side: it has worsened the following day (9 July 2022).

Without getting too technical, we can see that insecure top line, which includes web facing (A), canonical name (CNAME), mail exchange (MX), start of authority (SOA) and Text (TXT) are included. We have gone from five insecure DNS Records to six. There is parity of a single DNS Delegation issue, and Errors have increased by one. Most important of all is we have literally gained five Warnings on the day of the incident and in the following 24 hours.

When we started researching into the warnings, we found the following:

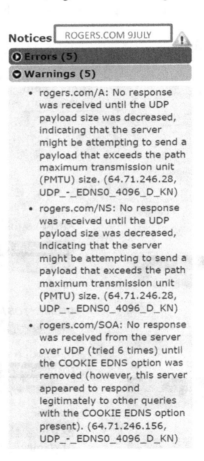

I want to draw your attention to the following: You do not need to be a DNS expert; however, as I always try to simplify things, think of DNS as a Post Office and content delivery network (CDN) as a Fedex or DHL distribution network. The only difference is that in the DHL world they deliver physical 'packets'; in the digital world, digital 'packets' are delivered. In both cases, security throughout the entire journey, from collection to ultimate delivery, is paramount from the initial sender to recipient. If your DHL delivery arrived broken, clearly opened and damaged, you might be rather annoyed, and equally so if it did not turn up at all. The same applies for digital communications and data.

> Rogers.com/A: No response was received until the UDP payload size was decreased, indicating that the server might be attempting to send a payload that exceeds the path maximum transmission unit (PMTU) size.

The above is commonly known in the DNS and cyberworld that understand DNS as potential data exfiltration. Digital packets are the payload and DNS requests are typically quite small, hence the small nature of the PMTU. When the payload exceeds the payload size, it is a clear indicator that somebody is trying to increase (piggy-back) data on the packets without being noticed. These urgently require checks as they are what is known as Indicators of Compromise (IOC).

There are two main types of data exfiltration via DNS. The first is a steady trickle, where data is being gathered and collected over a long period of time. We call this 'Living off the Land'. This is the norm for State Nations who are in no hurry to amass data for future use. Such attacks can, when undetected, go on for years: the more data the better. Then there are the Ransomware Attacks where it is more a case of 'Smash and Grab' to exfiltrate as much data as possible quickly. The perpetrators can then take the data, often unencrypted data due to basic security oversights, and hold their victim to a Ransom payment.

Within several hours, at 21:48 on the same day, Rogers had managed to identify the DNS errors and warnings; however, the damage had already been done. What is clear is that Rogers, like the vast majority of organisations, lacked controls, management and governance of all DNS positions, only panicking, knee jerking and addressing some of these issues whilst in panic mode like a driver checking tyres after a blow-out.

As of today, 26 October 2022, I can confirm that Rogers' DNS position is still woefully Insecure, exposed, vulnerable and exploitable. This is NOT security by design but guarantees Insecurity by default.

Until the world awakens from its own ignorance of basic Internet security controls, management and governance, the game of cyber 'Whack a Mole' will continue unabated costing governments, economies and the citizens of the world.

If a clever person learns by their mistakes and a wise person by the mistakes made by others, then what is a person known as who refuses to learn from either?

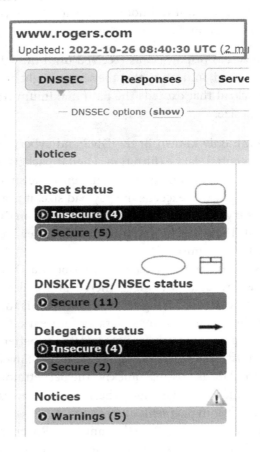

Index